Rafael López-Pedraza

HERMES AND HIS CHILDREN

Rafael López-Pedraza

HERMES
AND HIS CHILDREN

DAIMON
VERLAG

An earlier version of this work was published by Spring Publications in 1977, ISBN 0-88214-113-9. The present edition has been completely revised and expanded by the author.
All quotations and illustrations are acknowledged in the relevant places. References to Jung are from the *Collected Works* (CW) of C.G. Jung (Bollingen Series XX) translated by R.F.C. Hull, edited by H. Read, M. Fordham, G. Adler, and Wm. McGuire, Princeton University Press, Princeton, N.J., also published in Great Britain by Routledge and Kegan Paul, London.

Fourth Edition

ISBN 978-3-85630-735-6

Daimon edition Copyright © 2010, 2003, 1989 by Daimon Verlag, Am Klosterplatz, CH-8840 Einsiedeln, Switzerland

Cover design by Hanspeter Kälin:
Apollo and Hermes adapted from an original Greek image.

Photo of the author by Eddy Gonzales.

TABLE OF CONTENTS

Foreword

The most important terms in modern psychology, though originally based on experience, have become theoretical conceptions and, nowadays, are little more than jargon, the meaning of which is taken completely for granted. In this book, my rather personal use of some of these terms is related more closely to the image I am dealing with, a more direct expression of the psychic reading of an image.

Let us take, for example, the term 'psychic movement,' a term used consistently throughout the book. I consider that psychic movement is essential to a hermetic psychotherapy. More specifically, this term is of dramatic significance when we conceive of psychotherapy as devoted to moving, hermetically, that part of the psyche that has been paralyzed by the person's history or experience. It is not difficult, I believe, for the reader to imagine the complex mystery of illness in terms of fixation, paralyzation, or petrification. Unfortunately, in the course of his history, Western man has retained fewer and fewer ways to be initiated into his own psychic nature; initiation therefore became one of Jung's main concerns in psychotherapy: initiation into the repressed unconscious nature, which is fundamental to any healing. Now this is a view of psychotherapy in which Hermes, as the archetype of the unconscious, is the guide; most of the time, the only guide. For me, psychic movement lies not only at the core of psychotherapy, but also of life.

The way in which I use 'connect' and 'connection-maker' could perhaps be new for the reader. Hermes is known as the messenger of the gods; in other words, mythologically, he connects the gods and goddesses to each other and to man; thus he is the connection-maker. This is fundamental to an understanding of the variety of his appearances both in dreams, to which he gives his own significance, and in life, to which he gives his personal hermetic view. So when I use this term, it is with a very specific connotation. This book is based upon images, so let us imagine Hermes touching those spots where we are the most sorely afflicted, thereby connecting to them and, at the same time, connecting us to them. As the connection-maker, he gives us a new view of an episode in our lives, or of a pathology, which has been unconsciously dominant for too long. At the same time he reveals the psychic value in what had not seemed to be relevant or was hidden. In this way, Hermes is a god of transformation.

An understanding of the term 'archetype' is fundamental to the studies of Jungian psychology. However, I would be content if the reader is prepared to accept my personal view of this term: that Western culture is archetypal at its Greek cultural roots (Homer and Hesiod), and that the use of the term archetype in psychology and psychotherapy is an attempt to use the legacy of those two first poets. Following in the same Greek tradition, we can only say that psyche learns through the archetypes.

The above two paragraphs should, I believe, be sufficient to give the reader an idea of the way in which I use other psychological terms. I connect the term 'transference,' for instance, more to psychic movement than to its usual connotation. In the same way, psychotherapy, the book's main concern, is viewed within a conception that goes far beyond an analytical treatment: Our survival requires that we live our life as if it were a constant psychotherapy, to let our psyche have priority, to allow it to differentiate between what is psychic and appeals to its unique nature, and what is not psychic, and to allow it to live the feelings and emotions that nourish it. This is the most immediate way to connect to our nature, instincts, and history, and to the life we live. In other words, psychotherapy in this sense is an attempt to make life as psychic as we can, to keep our psyche in movement. If we fail we must suffer the consequences of a psychic disturbance, an illness, or the most common consequence of a repetitive and stagnant life.

Hermes and His Children is addressed to the therapist who intuitively feels that his practice depends on the encounter of two psyches propitiated by Hermes, psychic hermetic encounters, through which healing can come. This is the realm of Hermes: messenger of the gods, master of persuasion, master thief, guide of souls, teacher of Asklepios, and the therapist's inner companion in the solitude of his daily practice. It is in this realm that the therapist is liberated from the reductionism of preconceived theories and is differentiated from the many psychologies in today's world. It is here that psychotherapy is turned into a psychic creative work, where the therapist can begin to love his practice in the same way an artist loves his art.

Not least, this book is addressed to the general reader who, in his loneliness, feels the emptiness and stupidity of the times in which he is living, and who knows, secretly and hermetically, that some sense is given to his life in those scattered moments when Hermes, with his wand, mysteriously touches him.

Chapter I

Hermes – Psychotherapy – the Hermaphrodite

The premise of this book is to reflect the psychic dynamism of Hermes, this evasive god, in our daily lives. For this purpose, we shall turn to the classical legacy and to some scholarly works as well as to today's film-makers and the daily news of the world in which we live. As a psychotherapist, naturally my reflections come from my practice of a psychotherapy that gives a first rank to Hermes and whose main concern is with psychic movement: – either we move psychically or we stagnate. I want to give to Hermes and his sometimes odd imagery an essential place in psychotherapy, to connect a hermetic imagination to healing, and to conceive the therapist as an image-maker. This requires a psychotherapy that is aware of mythological expressions of the psyche, that looks into the person's conflicts with a mythical imagination. In other words, it is a psychology of the archetypes, bringing with it an obligation to improve upon the basic study of mythology and equate it with the study of psychology. This remains an immense field for exploration.

This approach is well within the tradition of Jung; he was the first to give importance to Hermes in psychotherapy through his interpretations of hermetic symbolism and his alchemical studies, work which led to a psychology of depth. He was also the first to introduce the study of the archetypes into modern psychology, thus opening new ways for seeing into human nature and new possibilities of which we are still only partially aware. Historically, an approach to psychology via the study of mythology has probably appeared with a wider spectrum and clearer perspective in the present generation of Jungian analysts, who are contributing more and more to the study of the archetypes. However, I want it to be understood that I am in no way proposing a 'technique.' The aim of a psychology based on the archetypes is to 'look through' a situation in order to encourage psychic movement rather than to merely reduce the patient's condition to its mythical counterpart. We need to read mythology and the scholars' works to provide ourselves with the necessary background from which to reflect and come closer to the constellations that can appear in psychotherapy. Throughout our reading of mythology we have to continually be aware of the relationship between psychology and mythology to guard against missing the mark with our psychotherapeutic insights or being too caught up in the similarities of the mythologems to the patient's situations.

Needless to say, I am not promoting either the study of mythology *in extenso* or in the academic sense. A psychologist has to be in tune with, or see through, this mythological background via his own psyche. I believe one's psyche can be imaginatively stimulated only by those myths akin to one's own nature, history, and personality, the myths one lives in relation to the basic complexes. New myths, appearing with new complexes (pieces of life), challenge the psyche to move, and when there is a response to this challenge, the psychotherapist gains new perspectives and attitudes for psychotherapeutic practice. But, at the same time, it is important to realize that there are archetypes so alien to the psyche of the analyst that when they appear in the analytical constellation, he can only do something with the patient who offers them if he is able to accept the task of learning from archetypal conflicts which are remote from his own archetypal configuration and experience of life; that is to say, until he becomes more acquainted with psychic elements which are unfamiliar to him.

Let us take a look at an old and very primitive appearance of Hermes as offered by a modern scholar. W.K.C. Guthrie begins his discussion of Hermes:

> ... [first] we shall listen attentively to the warning of Professor Rose: "We must not forget the possibility that the Arkadians found him in Arkadia when they arrived there, and that his name is not Greek at all." There will be more to say about this, but for the present we need only note that it is not beyond the bounds of possibility for the Greeks to have found and adopted an ancient indigenous god and given him a title of their own. Let us even note the opinion of Boisacq, that "l'étymologie de *Hermes* est inconnue." But having made these necessary offerings, we shall align ourselves firmly with Professor Nilsson when he declares, "The name is one of the few that are etymologically transparent and means 'he of the stone heap.'"[1]

It is evident in this exploration of Hermes' name, that for Guthrie, what Nilsson has to say is more useful than what Boisacq, with a knowledge which leads nowhere, tries to affirm. No image can come out of "inconnue." However, the "stone heap" is an image in itself, which can stir the imagination.

Guthrie precedes the above by informing us that, "It is tiring to be always treading the mazes of controversy."[2] Now psychologists, particularly in this sense, are not scholars. When reading the image of a god for psychology, we have to avoid those scholarly controversies which, in part, have to do with the personal history of the scholar, his time in the history of scholarship and his tendency to give too much importance to the historiography of the field he is working in.[3] Walter Otto, at the conclusion of his masterful portrayal of Hermes, gives us psychologists good advice about the

---

1. W.C.K. Guthrie, *The Greeks and Their Gods* (Univ. Paperback, Methuen: London, 1968), pp. 87-88.
2. *Ibid.*, p. 87.
3. Norman Brown, *Hermes the Thief: The Evolution of a Myth* (Vintage Books: New York, 1969), p. 3ff.

uselessness of falling into this kind of labyrinthine scholarship;

> In a concept of deity of such a sort there can be no purpose in differentiating between earlier and later qualities and in seeking for some line of development to connect the one with the other. Despite their multiplicity they are in fact only one, and if a single trait actually did come to the fore later than others, it still remains the same basic meaning which has found a new expression. Whatever may have been thought of Hermes in primitive times, a splendour out of the depths must once have so struck the eye that it perceived a world in the god and the god in the whole world.[4]

The first view of Hermes offered by our classical Greek scholars is as a "stone heap." The stone heaps were placed along the roads to mark them; they also marked the boundaries between villages, cities, and regions, landmarks fixing the boundaries and frontiers.[5] These heaps of stones, marking the geographical roads and frontiers, were also primitive altars consecrated to Hermes. The stone heap is, in fact, an archetypal image of a god. Therefore, we can say, this god, Hermes, "Lord of the Roads" as he came to be known, also marks our psychological roads and boundaries; he marks the borderlines of our psychological frontiers and marks the territory where, in our psyche, the foreign, the alien, begins.

Hermes made his epiphany as god of commerce at those primitive altars on the frontier. In former times, as well as today in our psyche, Hermes' commerce had elements of silence, cheating and thieving, always important ingredients in commerce and also in commerce with the unknown at the borderlines of our psyche. As we shall see later,[6] however, in this bartering or commerce at the borderline, Hermes can either guide the way or lead us astray.

---

4. Walter F. Otto, *The Homeric Gods,* trans. Moses Hadas (Thames and Hudson: London, n.d.), p. 124.
5. Brown, *Hermes the Thief, op. cit.,* pp. 34, 38-40.
6. See Chapter II on The Homeric Hymn to Hermes.

We are offered a further view of Hermes with his ithyphallic appearance [Plate 1]:

> The religious images erected to him were either in the 'Cyllenian' style, in which the image was a phallus of wood or stone, or else in that related style in which the image was a rectangular pillar with a head and an erect phallus – an image which in our language is called a herma.[7]

The ithyphallic herma is an image with a strong sexual component, expressing the sexual side of Hermes. Even within the limitation of these two primitive appearances of Hermes, the stone heap and the herma, we can assert that as well as being a phallic god strongly connected with sexuality, he is much more than this due to his stone heap appearance as lord of the roads. Throughout this book, one of my intentions is to offer the idea that our sexuality (so much the concern of this century's psychology) marks the roads we tread in life like milestones, that our sexual fantasies, images, and imagination participate in the psychological commerce at the borderlines of our psyche, marking the internal and external realms of life.

The above insights into Hermes, written ten years ago, have now been verified by Walter Burkert's contribution:

> It is not only the phallic sign that belongs to Hermes, but also the pile of stones; in fact his name 'Hermes' is derived from it: *hérma* is just a stone set up, hence *Hermáas* or *Hermáon*. This interrelation is explicable precisely from the signal function of both phallus and stone.[8]

He also takes us even further back, deepening our insights into Hermes, when he connects the herma to an observation from ethology:

7. K. Kerényi, *The Gods of the Greeks*, trans. Norman Cameron (Thames and Hudson: London, 1951), p. 171.
8. Walter Burkert, *Structure and History in Greek Mythology and Ritual* (University of California Press: Berkeley, 1979), p. 41.

Plate 1

… there are species of monkeys, living in groups, of whom the males act as guards: they sit up at the outposts, facing outside and presenting their erect genital organ.[9]

Here we are provided with a connection to Hermes that goes beyond the primitive end of the image – probably to that "ancient indigenous god," experienced by Guthrie, or those "primitive times, a splendour out of the depths," in the deeply romantic insight of Otto. Both confirm the classical scholars' attraction to Greek mythology as, in the words of Burkert, the most advanced among the archaic and the most archaic among the advanced. Burkert's observation from ethology allows us to include the animal in the most sophisticated and civilized archetypal images of Hermes – the connection-maker, the god of commerce, messenger of the gods, lord of the roads – and supports our intuition about the instinctual level in Hermes' activities and arts.

Burkert's contribution touches the living animal aspect of an archetype, which is different from an animal as an attribute of an archetype, such as the eagle of Zeus or the cow of Hera, or the sometimes spectacular appearance of monkeys in dreams, heralding unexpected movement and change in a psychological situation. Hermes' presence in us enables us to feel our own primitiveness, giving us a sense of instinct. This is essential to any insight into Hermes: an immediate sense of the reality of our being. It seems to me that this is how mankind, timeless man, has perceived Hermes.

Now that we have a first basic picture of Hermes, let us read a passage from Otto's *Dionysus* describing Hermes' strange and elusive character. This gives us the opportunity to read with interest a scholar's discussion of a concept and at the same time to steal and profit from a scholarly controversy so much in opposition to our reading of the image:

9. *Ibid.*, p. 40.

In origin, the god Hermes is supposed to have been nothing more than a protector, and the stone pillars and heaps of stones in front of farm houses and along the roads point to his presence. But all of the features which define his character: the paradox of his guiding and his leading astray, the sudden giving and taking away, the wisdom and cunning, the spirit of propitious love, the witchery of twilight, the weirdness of night and death – this diverse whole, which is inexhaustible and yet nowhere denies the unity of its being, is supposed to be only a complex of ideas which had gradually developed from the way of life of the worshippers, from their wishes and inclinations, ideas enriched by the love of story telling.[10]

Now, in the last four lines of this impeccable portrait of Hermes, we can see that the scholar moves from the imagery of Hermes into a conceptual language which distracts us from the image. However, in this passage, he gives us the opportunity to differentiate two ways of thinking – one mythical and image-making and the other conceptual. Otto, when he wrote this passage, was involved in a controversy, but we are not going to fall into the controversy itself: his portrait of Hermes, though shaped by a controversy, stimulates us into imagining the image of Hermes.

In this attempt to show how we can thieve from the scholars, there is also an attempt to delimit these two ways of thinking which tend to get confused. When the psychologist conceptualizes his thought, he can become involved in controversies and thus lose his own standpoint; whereas if he sticks to mythical thinking he stays more within the basic activities of the psyche. It is just as risky for a psychologist to concretize the findings of the scholars; his premise is psychical and his approach is to try to detect whether the material he reads from the scholars is attractive to his psyche, and whether he can find within it the analogies which would expand his psychotherapeutic vision. From my point of

10. Walter F. Otto, *Dionysus,* trans. Robert B. Palmer (Indiana University Press: Bloomington and London, 1965), p. 9.

view, to study the work of the scholars is to receive orientations and stimuli for my own psyche.

So bearing this in mind, our interest in Otto's passage is to gain an image of Hermes as protector. The passage also stimulated my imagination to see Hermes in his difficult position as the god of borderlines. We can see Hermes as a protector in the images of "the stone pillars and heaps of stones in front of farm houses and along the roads," and what was valid for the worshippers of Hermes in pagan times is still a valid metaphor in the psyche today. Furthermore, we can see Hermes as a god with a definite place as protector and helper in the difficult adventure of modern psychotherapy. In spite of Hermes' marginal, crooked, trickster, thief and cheater aspects, paradoxically, we can give full recognition to him in his role as a protector of psychotherapy. It is not a role that can be 'proved' (that would be a trap that has nothing to do with Hermes), but as we go along I shall try to make this apparent.

Let us imagine that Hermes himself provided the energy and inspiration for the enrichment of his mythology. Some of the stories in which he appears and above all, the "Homeric Hymn to Hermes" are going to be the sources of images for our study of Hermes in relation to psychotherapy. But we must bear in mind that together with the stories flourishing around this god, the earlier aspects of marking the road with its borderline, and his phallic side, as well as the implication of his being a protector, were always retained. His protection has its own meaning under Hermes' 'benison' and, as in life, it appears in psychotherapy within Hermes' complexities – "the sudden giving and taking away" – protecting the psychological movement of both analyst and patient within his borderline, a protection which never implies dependency or power.

To help further our psychotherapeutic reflection and gain more knowledge of Hermes' qualities, let us turn to Otto's unmatched rendering of him in his *The Homeric Gods:*

But his wonderful deftness makes him the ideal and patron of servants also. All that is expected of a diligent servant – skill in lighting the fire, splitting kindling wood, roasting and carving meat, pouring wine – comes from Hermes, whose qualities made him so efficient a servant to the Olympians.[11]

Then Otto continues, "Admittedly, these are no dignified arts …"[12] And, "If we compare Hermes with his brother Apollo or with Athena we notice a certain lack of dignity in him."[13] However, "Though the world of Hermes is not dignified, and indeed in its characteristic manifestations produces a definitely undignified and often enough dubious impression, yet – and this is truly Olympian – it is remote from vulgarity and repulsiveness."[14]

Otto is telling us that these two complementary qualities of Hermes – "diligent servant" and "lack of dignity" – in being truly Olympian, are archetypal. If, for a moment, we imagine a psychotherapist who insists too much on the dignified aspect of his personality, we can conclude, without much need of speculation, that he has little contact with Hermes. If we psychotherapists behave in too dignified a way in psychotherapy, then how can we contact the great percentage of patients who mostly come to the analyst in the first place to discuss the undignified episodes in their lives? Only the undignified Hermes in the analyst can constellate a communication with the undignified side of life and can evaluate hermetically what has been reported as undignified. Only this hermetic evaluation of the undignified (and here by 'undignified' we follow Otto when he puts it in opposition to the dignity of Apollo and Athena) in the other can provide the insights which could be of fundamental importance for psychotherapy. Psychotherapy is an undignified business and the constellation of this basic aspect of

11. Otto, *The Homeric Gods, op. cit.,* pp. 104-105.
12. *Ibid.,* p. 105.
13. *Ibid.,* p. 104.
14. *Ibid.,* p. 123.

Hermes has to occur at the level marked by this undignified side.

Close to the observations provided by Hermes' undignified side, is his role as the servant of the gods. The art of psychotherapy is a servitude. This servant attitude belongs to the classical Jungian tradition, in which the psychotherapist is merely the servant of the therapeutical process at whatever level the process moves.[15] Even though the idea of the therapist as servant is traditional, it does not mean that the therapist is a servant *per se;* on the contrary, it means a daily struggle with other aspects of the personality (archetypes with dignified characteristics) which would like to take over the psychotherapy. A dignified attitude is usually not one of servitude, and it can be seen in the context of being an identification with archetypal forms alien to that of just being a servant of the psychic process. For example, when an analyst prefers to stick to the dignified side of life he is no longer the servant and can thus be prone to identify with the archetype of the healer in its many manifestations; by insisting on his dignity he is less able to be a servant of the healing process.

It is important that, in our discussion of Hermes' undignified, servant aspect in psychotherapy, we bear in mind Otto's clear statement that, though Hermes is both servant and undignified, he is always "remote from vulgarity and repulsiveness." Otto advises us of Hermes' skill in dealing with the undignified; so when we discuss this aspect in terms

15. From my own psychotherapeutic experience, it seems that Hermes can be the servant of both the archetype of healing, centered in Asclepius (see Kerényi, *Asklepios: Archetypal Image of the Physician's Existence,* trans. R. Manheim (Bollingen Foundation: New York, 1959), and, in a more differentiated way, he can connect the patient to the archetype which made him ill, procuring healing by this connection. In actual practice I find little incompatibility between the healing constellation of Asclepius (the healer in the patient), and healing through the archetype in the complex which made the patient ill. The relationship between Hermes and Asclepius is well known. See Hermes' instructions to Asclepius in the *Hermetica,* ed. and trans. Walter Scott, Volume I (Dawsons of Pall Mall: London, 1968).

of psychotherapy there is no implication of vulgarity. Vulgarity is evidently alien to Hermes and would upset a Hermes' connection with, and evaluation of, this component which is called lack of dignity. I would say Hermes has a gusto of his own in dealing with the undignified side of the personality; his style and feeling can provide a psychological movement or unknot the dignified complexes compressing the patient's psyche. In psychotherapy today, one of the responses of an analyst confronted with a patient's undignified side is to try to constellate the patient's dignified side. We can suspect in this procedure a repulsion against the undignified. It is perhaps a repulsion against Hermes himself, expressed by way of introducing the dignified, an element belonging to another archetype, i.e., following Otto, Apollo and Athena, the archetypes that most represent the immediate values of the collective. This response misses the point and loses the possibility of a connection to Hermes through his undignified characteristic.

Returning to Otto, he says: "The world of Hermes is by no means a heroic world." And he attests to this with the following:

> An Odysseus and a Diomedes invoke Athena at their nocturnal enterprise, and the goddess comes. But Dolon, who is setting out upon a quite similar adventure during the same night but whose reliance is not on the spirit of heroism but rather upon craftiness, slyness, and above all luck, recommends himself, in Euripides' *Rhesus,* to Hermes, who is to guide him safe to his destination and back.[16]

Let us try to translate these lines of Otto into an approach for psychotherapy. The world of psychotherapy, particularly a psychotherapy concerned with Hermes, as well as being undignified and of servitude, is not a heroic one. If we consider psychotherapy to be an adventure – following Jungian tradition, an adventure into the unconscious – we realize that a heroic attitude is superficial for the demands

16. Otto, *The Homeric Gods, op. cit.,* p. 122.

of such an adventure. So Hermes provides imagery for the 'unheroic' attitude in the adventure of psychotherapy which, as we said before, depends on Hermes' protection and sometimes – why not? – on luck.

We reflected earlier on the tendency to identify with the healer archetype, but now we must be wary of a possible identification with the hero. In relation to psychotherapy, the emphasis of the identification would be on healing as a heroic deed, possibly one of the most inflated identifications of them all. This identification with the hero as healer has its own archetypal background – to mention just one example, Achilles performing a quick healing of Patroclus during the battle.[17] This is an image that gives us an insight into the healer as a hero, which today would be the military physician. It is nevertheless a healing metaphor that is inapplicable to a hermetic psychotherapy which aims at the adventure of moving someone along the roads in the psychic depths of the complexes. Not even in what could be seen as an emergency situation, for example, a psychotherapist receiving a patient in a clinical setting, would an attitude of the hero-healer be valid.

Otto says specifically that Hermes is the "friendliest of the gods to men,"[18] evidently a characteristic unique to Hermes. He "… is a genuine Olympian. His essence possesses the freedom, the breadth, and the brilliance by which we recognize the realm of Zeus. And yet he has properties which set him apart from the circle of the children of Zeus…"[19] Though Olympian, Hermes is different from the other Olympian deities. We have discussed his borderline aspect, a characteristic which in itself makes him different from the other gods, who seem to be the center of the specific aspects of life to which they give their imprint. Hermes permeates

17. In Michael Grant and John Hazel's *Who's Who in Classical Mythology* (Weidenfeld and Nicholson: London, 1973) there is a plate of a "red-figured bowl from Vulci (Etruria) c. 500 B.C." This plate shows "Achilles tending the wound of his friend Patroclus."
18. Otto, *The Homeric Gods, op. cit.*, p. 104.
19. *Ibid.*, p. 104.

the whole world because of his ability to make connections. From his borderline, he connects to the spheres of the other gods and has psychic commerce with them. He is the connection-maker and he is the messenger of the gods.

Hermes' borderline aspect favors his friendliness, or, to put it in more archetypal terms: he is the friendliest to the other gods. He does not fight with the other gods and goddesses when they are busy fighting among themselves.[20] Hermes has no need to fight for his center; he does not have one. If we internalize Hermes' friendly side, then it is Hermes in us who befriends our psychological complexes centered by the other gods. We can imagine a person going along the roads of life (or psychotherapy) protected by Hermes, at times in fear of the road, its darkness, and its desolation. We feel afraid of our solitude; we feel alone more often than we realize. It is in precisely these moments that Hermes makes his epiphany, when we feel that instinctual primitiveness mentioned in the first part of this chapter, when our prayers go to Hermes and in praying we feel his friendly side. Robert Creeley's poem "Prayer to Hermes" is an epiphany of Hermes in this sense; here are the opening verses:

> Hermes, god
> of crossed sticks,
> crossed existence,
> protect these feet
>
> I offer. Imagination
> is the wonder
> of the real, and I am
> sore afflicted with
>
> the devil's doubles,
> the two's, of this
> half-life,
> this twilight.[21]

20. *Ibid.*, p. 105.
21. Robert Creeley, "Prayer to Hermes" in *Spring* 1980 (Spring Publications: Dallas, 1980), p. 60.

The poet confirms the feeling that Hermes is a friend in the desperation of our solitude; and he brings not only companionship but his hermetic connections to our conflicts, keeping the complexes in movement and enabling psychic life and psychotherapy to unfold.

To describe the duplexities of the god, Otto uses the analogy of night: "Danger and protection, terror and reassurance, certainty and straying – all these night conceals within herself."[22] Of Hermes himself, he says: "It is in his nature not to belong to any locality and not to possess any permanent abode; always he is on the road between here and yonder…"[23] With these lines Otto gives us the very essence of Hermes' nature, probably the one among his many qualities that most challenges us when we are faced with conveying it into a therapeutic insight. It is here in this duplexity of being "always on the road between here and yonder" that Otto offers us another image, closer to the psychic than that of the boundary stones, for giving insight into the concept of the borderline. In the borderline (the duplexity) there is no split, for instance, into day or night, "We sense the peculiar twilight mood, and though the time is daylight, we think of the uncertainties of the night…"[24] All these elements – the duplexity, being in the here and yonder, and the twilight mood – move us toward archetypal references for what psychiatry and psychotherapy have coined as a 'borderline' condition. We have an imaginative background of archetypal references for a pathological condition expressed with a concept. The psychiatric term 'borderline' condition can be seen as a pathological expression of this peculiar aspect of Hermes' borderline nature or being. We can see that condition of living life within a duplexity, half in a mental institution and half in the city,[25] half neurotic with psychotic spells, either as being an expres-

---

22. Otto, *The Homeric Gods, op. cit.,* p. 120.
23. *Ibid.,* p. 117.
24. *Ibid.,* p. 118.
25. Rehabilitation houses are even called 'half-way houses.'

sion of Hermes' pathology or as a manifestation of his true essence, something we have all experienced, being half-sick, half-healed and our lives moving along that road between sickness and healing.

Otto describes another way in which Hermes makes his epiphany:

> But the marvelous and mysterious which is peculiar to night may also appear by day as a sudden darkening or an enigmatic smile. This mystery of night seen by day, this magic darkness in the bright sunlight, is the realm of Hermes, whom, in later ages, magic with good reason revered as its master. In popular feeling this makes itself felt in the remarkable silence that may intervene in the midst of the liveliest conversations; it was said, at such times, that Hermes had entered the room... The strange moment might signify bad luck or a friendly offer, some wonderful and happy coincidence.[26]

And Otto's beautiful description allows us to make another theft from a scholar and move Hermes directly into the analytical consulting room. We have all experienced those remarkable silences. They can be detected as an epiphany of Hermes, expressing itself in this uncanny way, having its own significance and value.

These strange moments are the peculiar expression of Hermes. It is in these instances of his epiphany that he moves us the most, and his appearance impels us to remain silent; this is when he bestows most of his benefits, when he is the friendliest of the gods, when he connects us to our primitive instinct, when he introduces his own archetypal borderline world, or, better said, a world different from the world of the other gods. "It is in the full sense of a world, that is to say, a whole world, not a fraction of the total sum of existence, which Hermes inspirits and rules. All things belong to it, but they appear in a different light than in the

26. Otto, *The Homeric Gods, op. cit.,* pp. 117-118.

realms of the other gods."[27] We can already glimpse a world of immense importance for the art of psychotherapy.

Now I would like to continue by giving my own impressions of how Hermes appeared in the consulting rooms of the two main pioneers of modern psychology – Freud and Jung. We know that in Jung's legacy Hermes/Mercurius is important, and it would be unnecessary to count the innumerable references to him in the *Collected Works*. Jung was a hermetic man who had a deep understanding of Hermes' psychology, and Hermes' presence was evident throughout his life and along the road of his creativity. Jung left behind him a psychology which is largely hermetic in both conception and practice. It was more than likely Hermes who guided him into the alchemical vessel, where he found the container for his psyche and which made possible his experience of the soul. His exploration of the alchemical treatises gave him the necessary borderline from which he could explore the borderline in himself and, via Hermes, the many possibilities of the psyche. Alchemy is a psychology of the paradox, a borderline psychology, which implies that it can only be apprehended by way of Hermes' leading the way into the unconscious.

Jung insighted the alchemical treatise as an expression of a symbolical process (the process of individuation), in which symbols, expressing oppositions in unconscious contents, mark the road along the alchemical opus and, in the same way, mark the road along the analytical process of individuation, a process which expresses itself paradoxically. Jung wrote: "As Mercurius is the principal name for the arcane substance, he deserves mention here as the paradox *par excellence*."[28] And he began his chapter on the Paradoxa thus: "The tremendous role which the opposites and their union play in alchemy helps us to understand why the alchemists were so fond of paradoxes. In order to attain this union, they tried not only to visualize the opposites

27. *Ibid.*, p. 120.
28. *CW* 14, para. 38.

together but to express them in the same breath."[29] He then
proceeds to give a picture of what was going on in the souls
of the alchemists with many examples of their paradoxical
statements, which show how the paradox held both spiritual
and pathological complexities. In a footnote with reference
to the above we can read a piece of Bonus' treatise and see
how an alchemist expressed the paradox:

> Wherefore whatever they are able to say and declare concern-
> ing virtues and vices, concerning the heavens and all things
> corporeal or incorporeal, the creation of the world ... and of
> all the elements ... and concerning life and death, good and
> evil, truth and falsehood, unity and multiplicity, poverty and
> riches, that which flies and that which flies not, war and peace,
> conqueror and conquered, toil and repose, sleep and waking,
> conception and birth, childhood and old age, male and
> female, strong and weak,...[30]

As we have implied before, it was not Jung's capricious
choice to immerse himself in the alchemical treatises. We
suggested that it was Hermes, lord of the roads. who stirred
his curiosity and led him into alchemy – to "Make Mercury
with Mercury."[31] Alchemy was part of his own historical
tradition and centered the conflict in this Swiss man studying psychology at the beginning of the century; Jung had a
particular religious inheritance, a family pathology, a hunger for erudition and cultural knowledge, plus the Medieval
rootedness of his Swiss soul. In alchemy he found the
symbolized imagery from which he could see through into
his own self and the world. Jung's attitude enabled him to
accept Hermes with his complexities, to accept Hermes'
epiphany and guidance along the unknown roads of psychotherapy. For Jung, psychotherapy became a borderline hermetic business (paradoxical). Hermes made a definite
appearance in the analytical consulting room of C.G. Jung.

29. *Ibid.*, para. 36.
30. *Ibid.*, para. 42, note 1.
31. *Ibid.*, para. 37.

No matter what conception we have of the alchemists and their historical contribution, we recognize that their work provided them with the tools for looking into the unconscious, for working on their psychic projection, for moving their psyches, and for containing their madness. Because of Jung we can now recognize what fine psychologists they were; they have helped accustom our eyes to look into what is called the unconscious. We psychologists need this exercise in order to train our perception and become familiar with the language of the unconscious, in this case, the language of the alchemical hermetic borderline. This training in alchemy teaches us to be more or less able to understand a patient's series of alchemical dreams and to get used to the borderline from where we can see the other's psychic material. When we 'see' the material and can track down the symbols and images with some accuracy, we are already in psychotherapy. Through reading alchemy, we become acquainted with the images and symbols, so strange and alien to the conscious personality, presented by the unconscious. We become more familiar with the awkward, horrifying and sometimes terrorizing aspects of the unconscious. We assume they are expressions in human nature trying to compensate that same nature. The basic 'stuff' of psychotherapy is reflection upon images; following Jung, it is an instinctual reflection and, at the same time, a happening. Jung repeatedly said that psychotherapy is indeed an art; but it is an art developed out of the instinct of reflection. Here we can begin to see psychotherapy as a workshop of images, led by the psychotherapist's craftsmanship and art as image-maker.

Turning now to Freud – though let us keep him more as a historical bas-relief – we can see that, in spite of Freud's scientific orientation, Hermes, the most psychological of the gods, also made an appearance in him. Freud was a nineteenth-century Jewish, Viennese, 'Victorian' man. His psychological discoveries at the turn of the century were pervaded by the complexities of natural science at that time, the sexual prudishness of the era, and the patriarchal, monotheistic fantasies of the Jewish tradition.

When Freud was constructing his theory of sexuality, it is doubtful whether he thought for a minute that, within his Jewish tradition, he was also dealing with repressed pagan gods. He and his followers were convinced they were studying one more of the many natural sciences being studied at the time. Thus their point of observation was focused on the organic, biological, physical side of sexuality, and their main theory connected mental illness (hysteria and neurosis) with sexuality. They saw the complicated disturbances in sexuality as having a cause-and-effect relationship with the illness they were studying. Evidently, they were not aware that in sexuality there are gods, particularly Hermes, the connection-maker, but also instincts and history. So any conception we might have of sexuality and, needless to say, any theory of sexuality, cannot be seen only in terms of a personal history. Each god has a particular sexuality. The pagan view of sexuality – all the various forms – implies polytheism / polymorphism, a view conflicting with Freud's monotheistic Jewish religious heritage.[32] These pioneers of modern psychology were not aware that, in their great discovery of sexuality as a field of research, at least one pagan god was intervening in their psyches, a pagan god with an ithyphallic appearance who is the messenger of the gods, the connection-maker who is able to connect to the other gods' sexuality. Repression was a personal matter and they were not at all aware of the history of Christianity as a represser of sexuality and the emotional body. They even confused (their followers still do) these two main levels of psychic repression. And, of course, they were not aware of the repressive times in which they were living (Victorian), nor were they aware of repression in their own Jewishness.

32. Throughout the book I shall bring more material in this connection. See also: "On Cultural Anxiety" in *Symbolic and Clinical Approaches in Practice and Theory: Proceedings of the Ninth International Congress for Analytical Psychology, Jerusalem, 1983,* Eds. Luigi Zoja and Robert Hinshaw (Daimon Verlag: Zurich, 1986).

The historical and religious backgrounds of our pioneers prevented them from keeping the borderline between the organic, physical penis and the phallic imagery of the god, not to mention his role as lord of the roads. All their energy went into working out a theory of penis-libido-sexuality which, archetypally, can be connected with Hermes. And so this god who, among the many aspects of his nature, does not want to be caught in serious scientific studies, scattered himself like a piece of quicksilver and dispersed himself, making those serious, scientific, late Victorian pioneers of modern psychology see the focus of their attention, the penis equated with sexuality, symbolized everywhere [Plate 2]. Their seriousness blinded them to Hermes' grace, foolishness, and oddity in sexuality; they were unable to accept the undignified, twilight, unscientific, borderline appearance of Hermes. Their attitude resulted in a psychology of the ego, with an ego sexuality. Hermes' borderline could not appear in their stressing of the split between the ego and what they called the id. All the rich possibilities of psychic life were blocked because there was no connection to them from a favorable borderline. Borderline was now threshold and censor. Psyche, as man's soul, disappeared from the studies of psychology; it became not the study of the psyche and its movement, but the fantasy of an ego-centered psychology backed by preconceived ideas and techniques. Sexuality was seen as an ego activity and the borderline, where Hermes can appear both sexually and as connection-maker, was coined as a term only to mark the boundaries of the psychical frontier over which the ego could not pass. In his psychoanalysis, Freud did the only thing he could do: to repeat the history of psychic repression of the Jewish people.

In contrast, Jung had found Hermes through his study of Gnosticism, fairy tales (*The Spirit Mercury*), anthropology, and, as we have already discussed, alchemy; Hermes became what might be called the matrix of his psychology. Once Hermes' symbolism and imagery had become a basic part of Jung's studies, the borderline he marks supported an atti-

Plate 2

tude which opened up the possibility of studying depth psychology. It opened the way, as well, for viewing sexuality from that very borderline of Hermes, where, besides the personal physical aspect, it could be seen in terms of the impersonal archetypal connections made by Hermes. Sexuality then became not only the traumatic cause of mental illness to be cured, but a valid expression among others of man's psyche. Sexuality – its traumas, inhibitions, fantasies, and imagery – became more an element of possible transformation of the soul than a localized sickness that paralyzes or petrifies the psyche.

To have an impression of the religious, racial, geographical, and historical conflicts in the psyches of Freud and Jung helps us to deepen our insights into the legacies they bequeathed, their methods, systems, psychological conceptions, etc. Now we are going to consider an episode in their lives which, besides being relevant to what I have been trying to say, offers further reflections on another appearance of Hermes.

Jung's break with Freud has always had the tone of a break between father and son or master and disciple; it has even been regarded in terms of dissidence, a view from which we can detect the poverty in the way in which some people view the separation. But let us read what Jung has to say about their mutual dream analyses during a trip to the United States in 1909:

> We were together everyday, and analyzed each other's dreams. At the time I had a number of important ones, but Freud could make nothing of them. I did not regard that as any reflection upon him, for it sometimes happens to the best analyst that he is unable to unlock the riddle of a dream. It was a human failure, and I would never have wanted to discontinue our dream analyses on that account. On the contrary, they meant a great deal to me, and I found our relationship exceedingly valuable. I regarded Freud as an older, more mature and experienced personality, and felt like a son in that respect. But then something happened which proved to be a severe blow to the whole relationship.

Freud had a dream – I would not think it right to air the problem it involved. I interpreted it as best I could, but added that a great deal more could be said about it if he would supply me with some additional details from his private life. Freud's response to these words was a curious look – a look of the utmost suspicion. Then he said, "But I cannot risk my authority!" At that moment he lost it altogether. That sentence burned itself into my memory; and in it the end of our relationship was already foreshadowed. Freud was placing personal authority above truth.[33]

Jung's description of these two men interchanging, discussing, and interpreting each other's dreams gives us a rather naive picture of two men, who at that time in their lives, were interpreting each other's dreams without knowing much about the implications of such an activity. For some years, they had been discussing the discovery of the phenomenon of transference, but their discussions were based mostly on the material provided by their patients and so they had a scientific external view of the phenomenon. They seem not to have realized that to tell their dreams to each other, on a ship travelling between Europe and America as a setting, implies a transferential situation, which inevitably contains an affective emotional tone. But our interest is to gain insight into how Hermes appeared in the flesh of the history of modern psychology during those dream sessions on that ship. We are also given a glimpse into both men's psyches and the repercussion the episode between them had on the basic legacy of modern psychology.

Freud, unconsciously backed by his race, religion, and history, showed his style of transference through his authoritarian, patriarchal, Jewish fantasy. Jung experienced the transferential impact of the meeting in another way. If he tried to approach Freud's dream as his equal, it was because

33. C.G. Jung, *Memories, Dreams, Reflections,* ed. Aniela Jaffé, trans. R. and C. Winston (Collins and Routledge & Kegan Paul: London, 1963), p. 154.

Hermes was already present in him, trying to guide the relationship and trying to see into the other's dream from his borderline. What we are calling Hermes' borderline implies a symmetry in relationship, a characteristic approach of Hermes, who is the "friendliest of all the gods to men." Moreover, Freud's insistence upon his authority and dignity does not go along with a hermetic psyche, does not suit Hermes, who is basically a non-authoritarian god. As we have seen earlier, Hermes is more concerned with the undignified side of the psyche, and this Freud was unwilling to expose.

Jung transferred in a hermetic way. Hermes in Jung's psyche sought the borderline approach to the other and to the imagery of the dream. Throughout the episode, Hermes as a way of transference was present in Jung. During the rest of his life Jung dedicated a great part of his work to putting the Hermes transference into words, symbols, and images. It is a transference which cannot be conceived of in terms of authority, power, system, or a reductive technique, because, to begin with, Hermes is not a technician and he eludes reduction by scattering himself all over the place, as he did in the case of the penis symbolism. Jung's alchemical opus gave us the first psychological lesson on Hermes' rhetoric[34] – Hermes expressing himself from his borderline in a language of his own, one that is very alien to the articulate language Freud bequeathed to modern psychology.

I would like to catch the image of the actual moment when Jung felt inside how, suddenly, the relationship with Freud broke. One feels a misuse on Freud's part of the word authority. I consider the situation had little to do with authority. Authority has a wider connotation, rhetoric, and feeling to deal with such a situation. There is no risk for a true authority in going psychologically into what would be personally shameful. Obviously Freud's dream contained shameful complexes and having no Hermes to deal with being 'cornered,' he blocked them, not with authority but

34. For fuller discussion, see Chapter VI on Priapus.

with power. Power is the most extreme aspect of the non-image, where instead of imagination there is only a barren wasteland. The Hermes in Jung sensed at once the power, and the possibility of any further relationship was destroyed. Certainly he felt this breaking up as a soul experience. From the way in which Jung relates this episode, we can insight the conflict in his personality: though he sensed the break hermetically, he expressed it in terms of his consciousness at that time, a consciousness that was the product of the Swiss collective consciousness, the Protestant religious background, and the fantasy of scientific truth, so dominant in those early years of psychological exploration. I see Jung in that moment caught in a conflict between the sudden hermetic detection of power, so intolerable to Hermes, and a consciousness imbued with the collective consciousness of the epoch.

The reader can have little difficulty insighting this scene of such key importance in the conception of modern psychology: on Freud's side the transference, constellating power in the analyst with a mere façade of authority, disguising his limited notions of human nature; and on Jung's, the sudden hermetic insight reflecting the emotional breaking of a relationship. Behind the scene are two different gods – the god of submission and Hermes, an inner god, who connects quickly to an inner happening and who does not submit, not even to his father. Evidently, the happening, so clearly described by Jung, was enough to make the break, though afterwards the relationship continued for some years, as if time is needed for the inner happening to repercuss in the outer aspect of the relationship, and for the final break to come about. This seems to be usual in the breaking up of a relationship, whether between lovers or friends or the psychotherapeutic relationship, in which the therapy continues even though the relationship is actually finished. It seems the psyche cannot accept immediately the reality of a break.

Probably Jung suffered a great deal in trying to make others understand his hermetic approach. The same boring criticism of his obscurity and lack of 'science' continues today, though he referred to this matter implicitly from the beginning. Some of his followers still attempt to find a 'scientific' background to, or proof of, his work. From this angle we can appreciate that, for Jung, discussions about transference, and even the word transference, were a nuisance. During his Tavistock Lectures he said:

> A transference is always a hindrance; it is never an advantage. You can cure in spite of the transference, not because of it. Another reason for the transference, particularly for bad forms of it, is provocation on the part of the analyst. There are certain analysts, I am sorry to say, who work for a transference because they believe, I don't know why, that transference is a useful and even necessary part of the treatment; therefore patients ought to have a transference. Of course this is an entirely mistaken idea. I often have had cases who came to me after a previous analysis and who after a fortnight or so became almost desperate. So far things had gone on very nicely and I was fully confident that the case would work out beautifully – and suddenly the patients informed me that they could not go on, and then the tears came. I asked, 'Why can't you go on? Have you got no money, or what is the matter?' They said, 'Oh no, that is not the reason. I have no transference.' I said, 'Thank Heaven you have no transference! A transference is an illness. It is abnormal to have a transference. Normal people never have transferences.' Then analysis goes on again quietly and nicely.[35]

And we can agree from the above that, yes, from the point of view of Hermes the need for transference, the dependence on transference, the handling of transference, transferential technique, etc. are indeed a nuisance. And in spite of this lesson one still sees so many Jungian analysts being terribly concerned about transference in terms of dependency. One is suspicious that they are probably more

35. C.G. Jung, *Analytical Psychology: Its Theory and Practice* (Routledge and Kegan Paul: London, 1968), pp. 169-170.

interested in power, with all its implications of dependency, than in the more psychic art of healing, which for me has to do with what Jung said in his Tavistock lecture. I would not have introduced the word transference in this paper had not Jung himself, using the same word, written a book called *The Psychology of the Transference*,[36] in which he broadened the picture psychology already had of a phenomenon that was being conceptualized within the narrowest concept. So, in this study of Hermes, let us keep the word transference and try to find new colors within the picture of this phenomenon. Jung's book on transference makes difficult reading. Nevertheless, by way of alchemical symbolism he takes us closer to a psychotherapy guided by Hermes. The alchemical treatise of Arnaldo de Villanova, and Jung's interpretation of it, express an awkward and obscure borderline condition. However, one feels a psychological movement within that borderline (or perhaps because of this very borderline situation) where Hermes placed both the alchemist who wrote the treatise and the psychologist who found in it elements through which to express the psychological movement of the transference.

What was seen by the alchemists and Jung in terms of symbols and paradoxes, we, in our practice, would like to see in terms of borderline and images. Today we are able to see this kind of condition, or pathology, that, historically, was veiled by the illusion of man's self-centeredness, his control of life, until this rational outlook collapsed and psychology was awakened. Today, we have to think in a way that our fathers at the turn of the century could not conceive of; we have to think in terms of borderline, images, and also the lack of images, which tells its own story. And we are more able to detect, diagnose, if you prefer, the extraordinary borderline spectrum of today with the help of instruments Jung devised – depth psychology, different insights

36. Now included in Jung's *Collected Works*, Vol. XVI, Princeton, 1958, 1979.

into man's madness more in accordance with the times in which we are living and the psychological needs of today. We see in terms of images because the plasticity of the image, in my view, provides a more favorable ground for reflection and provokes more psychotherapeutic movement than the language of the symbol. Yes, I am aware that a symbol can be a net to catch and gather the psyche, but also a symbol can halt the adventure of psychic movement, of exploring one's own nature and life.

If we follow Jung's line of the psychological process of individuation, we see that it is the transferential movement which carries it along. This transferential borderline movement is dominated by the Hermaphrodite, with all the accompanying references of the process – the King and Queen, the Fountain, the Water, the Child-soul, the Moon, the Wind of the Spirit, etc. But the central motif of this process is Hermaphrodite, a child of Hermes and Aphrodite.

The Hermaphrodite, a hermetic paradox, whose bisexuality reconciles the conflict of opposites, makes for a new awareness. I would say that all the attributes of Hermes we have mentioned so far are contained in the Hermaphrodite, which translates them into a complex language of its own. On the one hand, the Hermaphrodite offers its own field of reflection, and, on the other, its particular symbols and imagery (language) affect the analytical process of psychotherapy. I have in mind here not only the psychological movement the Hermaphrodite, with all the symbolism annexed to it, brings to the analytical process, but also those most difficult and complex cases, both men and women, who in the first hour of psychotherapy claim they are Hermaphrodites.[37]

With the Hermaphrodite, psychology begins to be psychology in the deepest sense. If we conceive of the Hermaphrodite as a particular consciousness in itself, then, from its own level of consciousness it apprehends that basic

---

37. See Chapter VI on Priapus.

reality of life which makes psyche possible: man and woman. The Hermaphrodite introduces us to the complexities of the masculine and the feminine within a unique symmetrical image. This image of the male/female opposition held within a symmetry has not been touched upon by any other school of psychology.[38]

The imagery of the Hermaphrodite gives a decisive indication of both the transferential and psychic movement in psychotherapy. However, in what we are calling transferential movement, we cannot leave out the necessary bisexual hermetic consciousness of the analyst, because in liberating the imagination from sexual polarities, it can constellate a psychological movement in itself neither male nor female. This kind of transference, which is not 'graspable' within the polarities and associations of 'man' and 'woman,' does not paralyze the complexes, rather it encourages a mercurial psychological movement; it has a connotation very different indeed from the connotation given to the transference by the Viennese pioneers of modern psychology. It is what makes the Hermaphrodite so profoundly important and fundamental to a psychology which, following Jung, does not need, or better said, tries to obviate a concrete transference, and which seeks to promote Hermes' transference with its possible result in the hermaphroditic synthesis.

This is by no means a simple matter for the analyst, considering that he has to insight the transference from the angle of Hermes-Hermaphrodite and to reflect the symbols and images coming out of the complexes in order to evaluate the transferential movement they bring, rather than the transferential conflict. This demands stamina and a delicate art from the analyst, since the imagery of the Hermaphrodite is usually repulsive. Hermes and the Hermaphrodite, as elements in psychotherapeutic work, have had little popularity – Hermes because he is so elusive and

38. This would be a more psychological answer to the feminist 'claim' that women are the same as men. In a hermaphroditic consciousness, men and women are equal.

undignified, and the Hermaphrodite because of the repulsiveness of its appearance in dreams, or in the claim to be a
Hermaphrodite.

In this first chapter we have been familiarizing ourselves
with some of the basic qualities, symbols, and imagery of
Hermes. Now we are concerned with one of his children,
the Hermaphrodite. Our intention is to try to read the
image, not the symbolism, of the Hermaphrodite with an
attitude that can improve our view of it even when its
imagery, though marking a psychological state in a patient,
abounds in grotesqueness repugnant to both patient and
analyst. Before going any further with our discussion, let us
look at the image of the Hermaphrodite as it appears in
Ovid's classical text, the *Metamorphoses:*

> How the fountain of Salmacis is of ill-repute, how it enervates
> with its enfeebling waters and renders soft and weak all men
> who bathe therein, you shall hear. The cause is hidden; but the
> enfeebling power of the fountain is well-known. A little son of
> Hermes and of the goddess Cythera the naiads nursed within
> Ida's caves. In his fair face mother and father could be clearly
> seen; his name he also took from them. When fifteen years had
> passed, he left his native mountains and abandoned his foster-
> mother, Ida, delighting to wander in unknown lands and to see
> strange rivers, his eagerness making light of toil. He came even
> to the Lycian cities and to the Carians, who dwell hard by the
> land of Lycia. Here he saw a pool of water crystal clear to the
> very bottom. No marshy reeds grew there, no unfruitful swamp-
> grass, nor spikey rushes; it is clear water. But the edges of the
> pool are bordered with fresh grass, and herbage ever green. A
> nymph dwells in the pool, one that loves not hunting, nor is
> wont to bend the bow or strive with speed of foot. She only of
> the naiads follows not in swift Diana's train. Often, 'tis said, her
> sisters would chide her: "Salmacis, take now either hunting-
> spear or painted quiver, and vary your ease with the hardships
> of the hunt." But she takes no hunting-spear, no painted
> quiver, nor does she vary her ease with the hardships of the
> hunt; but at times she bathes her shapely limbs in her own
> pool; often combs her hair with a boxwood comb, often looks

in the mirror-like waters to see what best becomes her. Now, wrapped in a transparent robe, she lies down to rest on the soft grass or the soft herbage. Often she gathers flowers; and on this occasion, too, she chanced to be gathering flowers when she saw the boy and longed to possess what she saw.

Not yet, however, did she approach him, though she was eager to do so, until she had calmed herself, until she had arranged her robes and composed her countenance, and taken all pains to appear beautiful. Then did she speak: "O youth, most worthy to be believed a god, if thou art indeed a god, thou must be Cupid; or if thou art mortal, happy are they who gave thee birth, blest is thy brother, fortunate indeed any sister of thine and thy nurse who gave thee suck. But far, oh, far happier than they all is she, if any be thy promised bride, if thou shalt deem any worthy to be thy wife. If there be any such, let mine be stolen joy; if not, may I be thine, thy bride, and may we be joined in wedlock." The maiden said no more. But the boy blushed rosy red; for he knew not what love is. But still the blush became him well. Such colour have apples hanging in sunny orchards, or painted ivory; such has the moon, eclipsed, red under white, when brazen vessels clash vainly for her relief. When the nymph begged and prayed for at least a sister's kiss, and was in act to throw her arms around his snowy neck, he cried: "Have done, or I must flee and leave this spot – and you." Salmacis trembled at this threat and said: "I yield the place to you, fair stranger," and turning away, pretended to depart. But even so she often looked back, and deep in a neighboring thicket she hid herself, crouching on bended knees. But the boy, freely as if unwatched and alone, walks up and down on the grass, dips his toes in the lapping waters, and his feet. Then quickly, charmed with the coolness of the soothing stream, he threw aside the thin garments from his slender form. Then was the nymph as one spell-bound, and her love kindled as she gazed at the naked form. Her eyes shone bright as when the sun's dazzling face is reflected from the surface of a glass held opposite his rays. Scarce can she endure delay, scarce bear her joy postponed, so eager to hold him in her arms, so madly incontinent. He, clapping his body with his hollow palms, dives into the pool, and swimming with alternate strokes flashes with gleaming body through the transparent flood, as if one should encase ivory figures or white lilies in translucent glass. "I win, and he is mine!" cries the naiad, and casting off all her garments dives also into the waters: she holds him fast though he strives against her, steals reluctant kisses, fondles him, touches his unwilling breast, clings to him on this side and on that. At length, as he tries his best to break away from her, she wraps him round with her embrace, as a serpent, when the king of birds caught her and is bearing her on high: which hanging from his claws, wraps her folds around his head and feet and entangles his flapping wings with her tail; or as the ivy oft-times embraces great trunks of trees, or as the sea-polyp holds its enemy caught beneath the sea, its tentacles embracing him on every side. The son of Atlas resists as best he may, and denies the nymph the joy she craves; but she holds on, and clings as if grown fast to him. "Strive as you may, wicked boy," she cries, "still shall you not escape me. Grant me this, ye gods, and may no day ever come that shall separate him from me or me from him." The gods heard her prayer. For their two bodies, joined together as they were, were merged in one, with one face and form for both. As when one grafts a twig on some tree, he sees the branches grow one, and with common life come to maturity, so were these two bodies knit in close embrace: they were no longer two, nor such as to be called, one, woman, and one, man. They seemed neither, and yet both.

When now he saw that the waters into which he had plunged had made him but half-man, and that his limbs had become enfeebled there, stretching out his hands and speaking, though not with manly tones, Hermaphroditus cried: "Oh, grant this boon, my father and my mother, to your son who bears the names of both: whoever comes into this pool as man may he go forth half-man, and may he weaken at touch of the water." His parents heard the prayer of their two-formed son and charged the waters with that uncanny power.[39]

Ovid's graceful rendering of the story of Hermaphroditus gives us an image remote indeed from the awkwardness of its alchemical symbolization and its invariable repulsive-

39. Ovid, *Metamorphoses,* trans. F.J. Miller (Loeb Library, Heinemann: London, 1916), Book IV, pp. 199-205.

ness in modern dreams and fantasies. Our attention is drawn by the difference of its depiction in Mediterranean mythical poetry and Medieval alchemy, as well as its modern appearance. This difference leads us to speculate as to whether the oddity and repulsiveness of its symbolizations and paradoxes is yet another historical expression of an archetype which has been repressed within Christianity. The appearance of the images, symbols, paradoxes, and fantasies around the Hermaphrodite are, following the classical Jungian approach, what we would call unconscious contents, elements very alien to the demands of the consciousness of daily life. When these elements arise in psychotherapy, they need to be contained, because the oddity they exhibit, due to their unconsciousness, tends to throw both the analyst and the patient off balance. As we shall see in a later chapter, these contents belong to a psychology removed from psychiatric and psychotherapeutic training, where these conflictive psychological elements are reduced to a psychiatric diagnosis, thus eliminating the possibility of the psychic movement contained in the imagery of the Hermaphrodite with its own consciousness.

It is always a challenge to contain and reflect the imagination of the Hermaphrodite because of its double duplexity. On the one hand it is bisexual, with an obscure pathology and, on the other, it is a psychic-mover. When confronted with the complexities of the Hermaphrodite, a hermaphroditic consciousness is essential in the analyst. However, there is another approach to all these difficulties especially for a psychotherapist interested in images and the imagination, and who feels that most of his practice depends on these. In Ovid's version of the Hermaphrodite he is offered an image of immense psychotherapeutic value.

The appearance of the Hermaphrodite since Medieval times presents an image that conveys a repugnant pathology, as we have said before, and thus we could call it an 'impossible' image [Plate 3]. When this impossible image of the Hermaphrodite arises in the patient, exhibiting its

Plate 3

strong pathology to the psychotherapist, it can alter or throw off balance the analyst's psychotherapeutic attitude and he can reject the impossible image or reduce it to the psychiatric point of view. Therefore, I want particularly to draw attention to the gracious beauty of Ovid's poetry, because it gives us a truly functional image for psychotherapy, a more accessible Hermaphrodite by way of a pagan poetic image, offering a purer hermaphroditic view than the conflictive Medieval symbolic one. Ovid's poetry and art offer what we could call a 'possible' image for the analyst to grasp [Plate 4]. He can make this classical image his own and thus be able to hold all the impossible, grotesque, repulsive, freakish imagination in the appearance of the Hermaphrodite with a classical image, which can be a guide and protection amid the whole confusion of the Hermaphrodite's strange appearance in psychotherapy.

The complexity of Ovid's image gives us many elements to reflect upon. After bathing in that uncanny pool with the nymph Salmacis, the beautiful boy, resembling Eros, realizes his new condition (the condition which gives its meaning to his name, Hermaphroditus) by feeling himself weakened. When the Hermaphrodite appears in psychotherapy, it is accompanied by a feeling of weakness in opposition to the illusion of strength of the male and female polarities, with the ingredient of 'machismus' they carry. It is a challenge for the analyst to insight this weakening. It is difficult to detect for what it is, in order to give it its proper value. It can too easily be pejoratively diagnosed as depression, the analyst being prone to see it in its pathological negative side rather than as a movement towards a new consciousness. This condition of weakness is essential for making possible the borderline hermaphroditic condition, which marks the psychotherapeutic movement from the old consciousness to a more psychological consciousness. Needless to say, the demands of society and the patient's environment which do not allow weakness, can be added to both the analyst's and patient's difficulty in evaluating the new hermaphroditic consciousness. Psychotherapy affiliated to the collective

Plate 4

consciousness tends to demand a realization in life mostly in opposition to weakness. Even in Jungian psychology the battle is for strength, coping, making decisions, responsibility, tough creative work, etc. Nevertheless, the component of weakness in the classical image of the Hermaphrodite introduces *in nuce,* an insight into the core of the Hermes/ Hermaphrodite transference: its achievement is weakening.

Moreover, the standard studies of Jungian psychology have little or nothing to do with the weakness achieved by Hermaphroditus in the pool. A Jungian trainee is required to analyze with both a male and a female analyst and there is the tendency to change analysts when the analysis seemingly no longer 'works.' Surprisingly, this move has never been discussed from the angle that it can upset and even split an archetypal image, or, at least, prevent the appearance of the Hermaphrodite which in itself contains both male and female, as well as what 'works' and does 'not work.' I am well aware that the 'achievement' of the Hermaphrodite in the pool, the prerequisite for hermaphroditic consciousness, is difficult for psychology to accept and find a place for in psychotherapy. Jungian psychology, just as in other activities of life, gives to weakness the usual derogatory connotation.

This might be the place to touch upon the so-called transference/countertransference. For our study of the archetypes we have to bear in mind that all the different gods, within their different psychologies, their different archetypal configurations, have their own way of transference; according to the alchemical view, each god or goddess has his or her own metal, water, fire, etc. Therefore, from an archetypal point of view, some messes of the transference/ countertransference could be seen as a situation in which the analyst reacts to the patient from an archetype that is not constellated analytically, the archetype constellated in the patient being a different one. Thus, by confronting the patient with a model he is unable to meet at the time, confusion is created, as well as more transferential dependency upon the analyst. Nothing is related to the indirection of Hermes, the connection-maker, nor to the Hermaphrodite with its possibility of bringing a new consciousness. There is no symmetric connection between analyst and patient and no proper connection made to the archetype constellated in the patient.

As a bisexual being, the Hermaphrodite, with its hermetic borderline nature in which sexuality and fantasy meet, is a psychic mover constantly prompting the transferential relationship we have to our complexes and pathology. This is not simply a curing therapeutic transference, but more the living of a lifetime in terms of transferential movement. Our memory, our relationships to others, our vision of the world, and of ourselves, metamorphosize in life. Explicitly, living life is more important than the illusion of a concrete achievement gained through psychotherapy.

If movement in life is what really comes out of psychotherapy, then the analyst's own movement in life is fundamental for enabling him to constellate life movement in the other; his transferential movement to his own complexes is the substance which brings about psychotherapy, not a fixed technique or a preconceived concept. We have found a new perspective from which to view the term 'transference.' It is movement in life. And here we have arrived at those questions the analysts of my generation ask themselves. Is my own analysis finished? Have I the energy to go back into a new analysis now that I am older? Is the relationship with my wife, and meetings with colleagues and friends to discuss our psychic movement enough? And to be more practical and precise: now, after some years, I am practising like this, but how am I going to practise in the future? So, always present is the question of how life is to be lived tomorrow, how our practice is going to be different today from yesterday.

Finally, let us read again the classical image of the Hermaphrodite in Ovid's *Metamorphoses*. Hermaphroditus, a child of Hermes and Aphrodite, very beautiful and resembling Eros, wandered out into the world and met a particular nymph, one who was not in Artemis' retinue or inter-

ested in hunting, but who liked to comb her hair and look
at her reflection in the waters of the pool to which she
belonged. Her sudden desire upon seeing the boy (fantasy),
and the boy's shyness and rejection of that desire, that game
played by nature between longing and rejection until the
'happening' while bathing in the pool, gives us a beautiful
image from which to reflect a constancy in the human
psyche. It is a fitting image for a psychotherapy which reverts
to life. This archetypal longing and rejection can be seen as
the dynamism which makes psyche and life move. It is,
perhaps, what animates transference, in terms of insighting
it as a constant movement in our psychological life. The
image tells us, in the prayer of the nymph and the boon
granted to Hermaphroditus, that our hermaphroditic consciousness, with all its peculiarities of borderline, twilight,
and weakness – which is never a so-called ego consciousness,
but one that keeps us going hermetically along the roads of
life – is constantly recreated by our longing and rejection.

Chapter II

The Homeric Hymn to Hermes

From the very day he was born in an Arcadian cave and from his first deeds, as recorded in the "Homeric Hymn to Hermes," we have an imagery of Hermes' nature that reveals the essential characteristics of this very evasive god. The Hymn tells us that at noon on the day of his birth, "...as he stepped over the threshold of the high-roofed cave, he found a tortoise there and gained endless delight. For it was Hermes who first made the tortoise a singer."[1] The Hymn goes on to tell how, after killing the tortoise, he ingeniously made a lyre out of its shell. Now for the study of psychology this might not have been of much importance at all, had not the story told us that with this lyre Hermes sang, as it were, the first of all songs:

> At the touch of his hand it sounded marvellously; and as he tried it the god sang sweet random snatches, even as youths bandy taunts at festivals. He sang of Zeus the son of Cronus and neat-shod Maia, the converse which they had before in the comradeship of love, telling all the glorious tale of his own begetting. He celebrated, too, the handmaids of the nymph, and her bright home, and the tripods all about the house, and the abundant cauldrons.[1]

The implication of this first act of Hermes seems to have

---

1. All quotations from "The Homeric Hymn to Hermes" are taken from *Hesiod: The Homeric Hymns and Homerica,* trans. Hugh G. Evelyn-White (Loeb Classical Library, Heinemann: 1914), p. 365ff.

gone virtually unnoticed in psychology and, of course, has been little reflected in psychotherapy. For Hermes' first response, in regard to what nowadays is expressed in technical terminology as the father and mother complex, was simply to connect beautifully to his father and mother. We all know that psychotherapy has tended to focus its main attention on the parental situation and, owing to this focus, Hermes has vanished out of psychotherapy. For the first thing Hermes did was to sing to his father and mother. Immediately, in the first moment, he connected to them properly, disregarding all speculations of positive and negative, the father and mother complex, the shame of parental sexuality, the guilt of being born out of love.

We have been discussing many aspects of Hermes and their importance for psychology. Now we are dealing more with the images of the god, and this particular image offers something of key importance for our study, which is to distinguish the obvious case history (father/mother) from how we are studying it here. Hermes' song to his parents tells us that what is 'obvious' does not belong to him, meaning the father-and-mother part of one's history. You could say it is obvious that he comes from a difficult parental situation. However, Hermes accepts his parents just as they are and does not let them make him more neurotic than he is.

Obvious, too, are the questions inherited from the medical case history that, without exception, psychologists ask the patient: What about your father and mother? What do you feel about them? After this type of question, the diagnoses appear – even more appalling to Hermes – that range from a 'deep' Oedipal situation to endless, commodious and superficial conceptions of the 'positive' and 'negative' father or mother complex. More often than not, the psychotherapeutic approach to this case history has been to overstress its importance, instead of taking it simply as a reference point, instead of deflating the unconscious importance given to the parental deities.[2] The case history can help us to learn a person's history, its components and complexes, and can be a useful frame of reference. But it is of more use in psychotherapy in that it enables us to detect, with Hermes' guidance, those elements in the patient that belong more to the nature that does not change,[3] as opposed to the patient's possible psychological movement.

If we think in terms of case history, we are seeing the parental situation, if at all, from the viewpoint of another archetype, but not from that of Hermes. Instead of making all that psychological fuss, in his first 'pass,' or you could say, first analytical hour, Hermes sang joyfully to his father and mother. He sang to them in spite of the fact that an analysis of his family 'case history' shows he had a somewhat neurotic father, even though he ruled Olympus. His mother, Maia, also could be said to have had a confused history. Her father was Atlas, and we know something of the inflation, neurosis, and depression of the Titan who has the fantasy of carrying the whole world on his shoulders.

Nevertheless, on the day he was born, Hermes sang to his parents with joy and, at the same time, in true Hermes style, a little mockingly. For me, this image could be a touchstone in psychology, because it gives the opportunity to amend the unnecessary abuse of seeing the father/mother complex as the metaphor 'chosen' to express 'neurosis.' This viewpoint, so exaggerated and at the roots of twentieth-century psychology, comes from other archetypes[4] and the imagery of Hermes the connection-maker, the one who can make his own connection to the parental, historical, psychic reality (complex).

After Hermes sang that first song of all songs, the Hymn continues:

2. For a reflection on case history, see James Hillman's essay "The Fiction of Case History: A Round" in *Religion as Story* (Harper & Row: New York, 1975).
3. See Chapter IV, fn. 18.
4. Hephaestus would be an archetypal example of resentment towards the parents; cf. Homer, *The Odyssey*, trans. E.V. Rieu (Harmondsworth: Penguin, 1946), p. 130.

But while he was singing of all these, his heart was bent on other matters. And he took the hollow lyre and laid it in his sacred cradle, and sprang from the sweet-smelling hall to a watch-place, pondering sheer trickery in his heart – deeds such as knavish folk pursue in the dark night-time; for he longed to taste flesh.

This part of the tale, telling of Hermes' trickery and desire to eat meat, begins to further our insights into Hermes' psychology. The first view of the world beyond his cave, the scenery he saw from the watch-place, was perhaps a mirror in which he reflected his tricky nature. The image seems to make a connection between his tricky nature and his longing to eat meat, and this is the focus of my interest and concern. Out of pondering upon his crafty nature came his desire to taste flesh, as if the two had a deep and primordial connection. The myth points to a past in the origins of mankind, a past of primal concern to modern scholarship which has given great attention to the search for food and the killing of animals with man's invention of the wooden spear, hardened in fire. Apart from speech, it is this which differentiates man from the other animals: anthropologically speaking, man is the animal that kills other animals with weapons, thus upsetting the ecology of life on earth. The treatment of these mythological complexes by such scholars as C.S. Kirk and W. Burkert, upon whose works I base my reflections, enables us to feel the Greeks' unique connection to this basic conflict at the root of culture.[5] Now, according to the Hymn, it is Hermes who, with his graceful trickery, can connect to such dark complexes. Here let me quote a passage from Burkert which moves into a reflection of the living actuality of these basic complexes in mankind:

5. G.S. Kirk, *Myth: Its Meaning and Functions in Ancient and Other Cultures* (Cambridge University Press: Cambridge, 1970); Walter Burkert, *Structure and History in Greek Mythology and Ritual* (University of California Press: Berkeley, 1979).

Still the historical perspective, while preserving the thrilling story, brings home a message about the situation of mankind which is not entirely antiquated. Rescued from a dead end by the use of violent technology more than once, man has triumphantly survived, but remains endangered by the curse of violated matter. The antithesis of nature and culture is more than a logical game; it may be fatal.[6]

Burkert's lines warning of the danger to the survival of mankind are chilling indeed.[7] For me, his insight is a masterpiece in the studies of Jung's theory of the complexes and valid for assimilation into the studies of psychology. We sense that he too is overwhelmingly involved in these complexes and that any attempt to gain an attitude of distance would fall into reduction.

In the "Homeric Hymn to Hermes" there is an evocation of the dark night-time of man's past. Scholarship conceives the basis of culture, i.e., religious ritual and mythological thinking, as products of the search for food. I would say that killing animals with weapons, religious ritual, and mythological thinking together compose a basic and conflictive complex in humankind. It is amazing how the "Homeric Hymn to Hermes," the product of a peasant mythological poetry (The School of Beoetia), has an intuition of that 'dark night,' and presents it with a grace and humor that has no parallel in other myths of this sort, making it easier to reach the average modern reader and thus more suitable for psychological study and reflection.

6. Walter Burkert, *Structure and History in Greek Mythology and Ritual,* p. 34.
7. Jung warned of the fatality of the eventual over-population of the world, a concern based on the excess of procreation leading to its own destruction. My paper "Moon Madness – Titanic Love" in *Images of the Untouched* (Spring: Dallas, 1982), introduced excess as a titanic component in human nature. We are living in times of ever increasing excess, which is unreflective. Burkert's warning can be taken as complementary to Jung's: Jung referred to excess in the present pointing to the future, whereas Burkert points to the continued presence of the oldest complexes (the dark night-time) in mankind, which are at the base of the conflict between nature and culture.

In our psychotherapeutic practices, we are used to seeing what possibly has a connection to these complexes: pathology at the level of the instinct of hunger – from obesity to anorexia nervosa, ranging from mild cases to the most severe and destructive. These cases tax the analyst's imagination, rendering him helpless in the face of such pathologies. For instead of an instinctual and archetypal regulation for survival, there is madness. Let me briefly make a comparison here: in psychosis and schizophrenia, we are sometimes able to detect an archetype, albeit unregulated or broken, but in the case of anorexia nervosa I, at least, am unable to have such a conception. To catch a glimpse of what is going on in the nature of these cases, we need to have a mythical approach like that of Walter Burkert, or an imaginative one like that of the psychosomatologist Alfred Ziegler. The latter conceives anorexia nervosa as an upward movement, which began in the Paleolithic Era, a time in which, as the archeological findings have demonstrated, goddesses were worshipped whose figures are models of obesity.[8] If Ziegler stirs our imagination with his notion of an upward ascetic movement, he also allows us to conceive certain cases of obesity in terms of a nature in which something remains at the level of the paleolithic complex, their bodies having a similar shape to those goddesses whose image Ziegler has observed so well:

> The appearance or, rather, the shape of these primal mother or feminine cult-figures often borders on the grotesque: the trunk is extremely full and corpulent, the posterior formed into overwhelmingly fatty buttocks (steatopygia). The figures seem to point to the position of reverence accorded eating and the material in general, including possessions.[9]

To return to the Hymn, the above reflections could also be applied to the repeated impression of there being a strong pathological component in the phobia for, or the

8. Alfred Ziegler, *Archetypal Medicine* (Spring: Dallas, 1983), p. 101.
9. *Ibid.*, p. 101.

rejection of eating meat, as if these very conflictive archaic complexes were finding an expression. When reflecting upon people who do not eat meat, its exclusion suggests an exclusion of Hermes in their psyche and, of course, of his psychological connection-making. Their pathology reveals a distortion in, or a lacking of relationship to the flexibility and versatility of this archetype (lacuna). The student of psychology who has had the opportunity to observe cases of this kind will have noticed other factors in the pathological picture: a fantasy of purity and cleanliness, a rigidity, a feeling of superiority, a guilt-making projection upon meat-eaters, and a lack of consciousness of any cruelty and destructiveness in themselves. The image of Hermes' need to eat meat suggests that when archetypal images which can connect us to an instinctual eating are missing, then eating becomes a system, paranoic if you want. But we must also be aware that this sort of paranoic system could also be seen as an attempt on nature's part to 'hold' a deeper pathology, a view which tries to penetrate more profoundly into these complexities. In any case, when this syndrome occurs, there would seem to be a lacuna where Hermes and his trickery should have a place in the psyche.

The Hymn goes on to describe how Hermes fulfilled the first step in his desire to eat meat by using trickery:

> The Sun was going down beneath the earth towards Ocean with his horses and chariot when Hermes came hurrying to the shadowy mountains of Pieria, where the divine cattle of the blessed gods had their steads and grazed the pleasant, unmown meadows. Of these the son of Maia, the sharp-eyed slayer of Argus, then cut off from the herd fifty loud-lowing kine, and drove them straggling-wise across a sandy place, turning their hoof-prints aside. Also, he bethought him a crafty ruse and reversed the marks of their hoofs, making the front behind and the hind before, while he himself walked the other way. Then he wove sandals with wicker-work by the sand of the sea, wonderful things, unthought of, unimagined; for he mixed together tamarisk and myrtle-twigs, fastening together an arm-

ful of their fresh, young wood, and tied them, leaves and all, securely under his feet as light sandals.

So on the day he was born a very cunning thieving appears, perhaps one of the earliest kinds of theft – thieving or rustling cattle. There are many stories and ballads about cattle-thieving, which give us the primordial feeling of the dawn of culture and literature. Probably the tale is telling us about man's craftiness in moving cattle. We know through paleontology that his skill in rounding up animals in order to kill them was developed very early. My interest is to convey into psychology this activity of man at the dawn of culture and, my particular concern, psychological thieving, both backed by the same god, Hermes.

From the historicity of mythical literature, we can appreciate the grace of an imagination that presents a god behind the act of thieving. We can insight this same primordial force as being behind our own psychological thieving. The image of this first theft, and one committed against Hermes' own brother Apollo, allows us to speculate that psychological thieving is invariably done to someone who is close to us: in the tale the theft takes places within the kinship of brotherhood. One has to be close enough to thieve psychologically,[10] for one psyche to thieve from another.

We are going to steal from the images in the "Homeric Hymn" the contents we need in order to insight the Hermes in a psyche thieving from another. Let me put it differently: Hermes in us is reading the Hymn, otherwise we would be

10. I would like the reader to collaborate with me and view psychological thieving as distinct from concrete thieving, though both are within the same metaphor and imagery. The motifs of thieving, Mafia assault, kidnapping, picking pockets, etc., frequently appear in dreams and can mean either a repressed content in the patient, who has at some time concretely thieved, or it can be a first appearance of Hermes as psychological thief, or even both. Neither plagiarism, mimicry, nor the obscure pathology of kleptomania have to do with the psychological thieving I am referring to, though they may belong to an aspect of this archetypal activity of Hermes. On kleptomania in relation to Hermes, see Murray Stein, *Midlife* (Spring Publications: Dallas, 1983).

reading it from the so-called ego (and then derive moral lessons from it about the shadow, etc.) or from another archetype, in which case we might read it as sheer nonsense, or as a piece of naive literature, or as a curiosity for a historical study.

The image of Hermes stealing cattle and the way in which he drove them led my imagination to connect this movement with a psychological thieving. In driving the cattle Hermes simulates a backwards movement, skillfully done by way of the sandals and inverting the hoof-prints of the cattle, a movement in one direction which appears as a movement in the opposite direction. I would like us to imagine this peculiar movement as the image from which to approach psychological thieving, a supposition very difficult to put into words. Psychological thieving belongs to the trickery of the Hermes psyche and is a thieving of basic importance for psychotherapy.

My reflections concerning Hermes' thieving were triggered by the importance Giulio Camillo gives to the sandals of Mercury, which he made into one of the Grades in his Memory Theatre.[11] Camillo says that the "Sandals of Mercury" Grade represents the natural activities of man – what man does by nature. Now what Hermes does with his sandals is to steal the cattle of his brother Apollo. It was from this that my insights developed into conceiving psychological thieving as a natural and basic activity of Hermes in the psyche. The imagery conveys, in the way he uses the sandals, how this activity of the psyche occurs. He simulates a backward movement. Psychologically, we can connect this image with Jung's conception of the backward movement of the libido. However I want to keep a distinction or borderline between backward movement of the libido and regression, even if this backward movement may be seen as similar to the psychological concept of regression. We could say it is the necessary regression into memory (personal and arche-

11. Frances A. Yates, *The Art of Memory* (Routledge & Kegan Paul, 1966), Chapter 6.

typal) that propitiates psychological thieving and brings
new insights.

We have to bear in mind the two sides of psychological
thieving. There is what we take from the other, such as a
profitable discussion in which we thieve the other's ideas.
And there is what Hermes steals for us from the complexes
and archetypes touched in our regression.

As described in the Hymn, Hermes' primordial creation
of his sandals is closely connected with thieving. How he
made and used the sandals gives us more insight into this
attribute than how the sandals appeared in later iconography of Hermes / Mercury, where they signified more Hermes as messenger of the gods and as god of commerce. The
Hymn makes the basic connection between the sandals and
thieving, just as Giulio Camillo did in his Memory Theatre
where he placed the "natural activities" of man in "The
Sandals of Mercury" Grade. For me, it is conceivable that
psychological thieving is a natural activity: thieving from
oneself and from another psyche.

This is where we can conceive of psychotherapy as
belonging within the natural activities of man, and not just
a superstructure of theories, concepts, and techniques.
Here I want to discuss how the natural activity of thieving
within a backward movement belongs to the analytical
transference. A great part of analysis is based on the hermetic possibilities in the analysand of thieving from the
analyst, and vice versa. We have been connecting this hermetic thieving to a retrograde movement of the libido,
which Jung insighted as leading the way towards psychic
development.

An analysis moves according to the potential the analyst
has for being stolen from. Jung was known to have said that
an analyst can help his patient just as far as he himself has
gone and not a step further. For the purpose of our discussion, Jung's statement can be paraphrased as: one can only
go on with a patient as long as one has something to be
thieved. For a constant thieving within the analytical transference, the analyst has to have enough in himself to be

thieved, and the Hermes part of his soul must accept hermetic thieving and its implied movement: retrograde movement. The favoring of retrograde movement brings about a reconnection to the different complexes, the different parts of one's history and memory. The concept of the analyst as a screen upon which the patient projects his psychic contents, or unconscious, does not fit into a Hermes model, at least not according to my insights concerning Hermes.

Hermes reached the byre in the meadow with his stolen cattle:

> Then, after he had well-fed the loud-bellowing cattle with fodder and driven them into the byre ... he gathered a pile of wood and began to seek the art of fire. He chose a stout laurel branch and trimmed it with the knife ... held firmly in his hand: and the hot smoke rose up. For it was Hermes who first invented fire-sticks and fire. Next he took many dried sticks and piled them thick and plenty in a sunken trench: and flame began to glow, spreading afar the blast of fierce-burning fire. And while the strength of glorious Hephaestus was beginning to kindle the fire, he dragged out two lowing, horned cows close to the fire; for great strength was with him. He threw them both panting upon their backs on the ground, and rolled them on their sides, bending their necks over, and pierced their vital chord. Then he went from task to task: first he cut up the rich fatted meat, and pierced it with wooden spits, and roasted flesh and the honourable chine and the paunch full of dark blood all together. He laid them there upon the ground, and spread out the hides on a rugged rock: and so they are still there many ages afterwards, a long, long time after all this, and are continually.

I would like to add this image of Hermes as the primordial man making fire to the line of thought we have been following: namely, the natural activities of man in psychotherapy. The image is profoundly moving in its expression and, undoubtedly, able to provide man – past, present, and future – with insight. We realize from the context of the

Hymn that a thief, a masterthief, made the primordial fire, and continues to make it as long as man is on earth.

The image of thieving, centered in the "Sandals of Mercury" Grade of Camillo's theatre, and the image of fire-making – both natural activities of man – are contrasted with the Prometheus Grade.[12] This is the Grade of another thief, a stealer of fire; but, in this case, he identifies with his theft, and goes into the inflation of thieving "For the benefit of mankind," as Aeschylus has Prometheus say in his tragedy. An archetypally oriented psychotherapy, more connected to the sources of life, has to be able to differentiate clearly between these two kinds of thieving.

To put it in other words: the most natural and hermetic psychotherapy is always confronted with Promethean historicity, leading to an inevitable conflict. As in other aspects of life today, psychotherapy lives the conflict between a Hermes consciousness and "Promethean knowledge."[13] The many new discoveries psychotherapy uses for the 'benefit' of the mentally ill patient – new psychotherapeutic techniques, insulin, electroshock, the latest pill – either conflict with the natural psychotherapy of Hermes, or can encourage a frame of reference, a container, for another appearance of Hermes in psychotherapy.

The last image in this passage is very beautiful. The poet touches the ineffable, as if he had an extraordinary consciousness of what he was writing about, as if he were already aware of the eternity of the imagery he was dealing with. He conveys how the image would be in man's memory for all time. He was writing about the archetypal memory of humankind, the memory behind our memory of a long-lived life and, more precisely, the memory akin to the children of Hermes.

---

12. *Ibid.*, p. 146.
13. Paolo Rossi, *Philosophy, Technology and the Arts in the Early Modern Era,* trans. Salvator Attanasio, ed. Benjamin Nelson (Harper Torchbooks: Evanston, 1970), Appendix III.

The next episode in the Hymn describes the way in which Hermes performs such an important thing as sacrifice. It gives us a clue to the ritual of sacrifice itself. The essential characteristics of a god are demonstrated by the way he performs sacrifice. A sacrificer to that god is given the sacrificial ritual by the god. The gods and goddesses each have their own rituals of sacrifice, and sacrifices made to each god or goddess connote their various characteristics.[14]

In discussing Hermes' sacrifice I am again going to introduce Prometheus as a counterpart. Prometheus was also a sacrificer, and he offers himself as a bas-relief from which to reflect our insights into Hermes' sacrifice.

> Next glad-hearted Hermes dragged the rich meats he had prepared and put them on a smooth, flat stone, and divided them into twelve portions distributed by lot, making each portion wholly honourable. The glorious Hermes longed for the sacrificial meat, for the sweet savour wearied him, god though he was; nevertheless his proud heart was not prevailed upon to devour the flesh, although he greatly desired. But he put away the fat and all the flesh in the high-roofed byre, placing them high up to be a token of his youthful theft.

The image of Hermes' sacrifice gives us a hint as to what could be called man's daily religious activities centered in the sacrifice. Sacrifice is a central religious motif, but it is also profoundly psychological. It seems as if religion, in terms of the way Hermes sacrifices, is so naturally internalized that it is difficult to distinguish the borderline where Hermes' psychization[15] is delimited from what we call religion. Perhaps his sacrifice provides the energy for a natural religious living, religion as a natural activity of man, 'religare' to oneself and others. For me, Hermes' sacrifice,

---

14. *Picatrix, Das Ziel des Weisen von Pseudo-Magrîti,* trans. Helmut Ritter and Martin Plessner (Warburg Institute: London, 1962) describes the sacrificial rituals required for the different Planets.
15. The idea of psychization comes from Jung, *The Structure and Dynamics of the Psyche, CW* 8, para. 234.

psychologically speaking, challenges any other model. It is the only model which can be conceived in terms of total psychization and internalization, providing a *rotatio* of the libido that keeps the psychic economy alive and in movement.

If we think of this sacrifice in connection with psychotherapy, the image gives us an insight into that daily sacrifice which Hermes in us constantly offers to all the gods, including himself, though – and this is the point – never identifying with the sacrificial offering. It is a constant sacrifice in which all the gods take their "wholly honourable" portion. With Hermes' honoring of the gods, we have an image for what might underline the word 'tolerance' in a way one can find nowhere else. I am giving to the word 'tolerance' both its common and utopian connotation. However, my interest is to introject its content for imagining the tolerance that Hermes' nature offers.

During our discussion of thieving, I referred to the "Sandals of Mercury" Grade in Camillio's Theatre confronting the Prometheus Grade. Both Hermes and Prometheus are thieves and both are sacrificers. These two models are in conflict in Western man, and only to be apprehended if we can differentiate them and accept that both are in our nature: two sacrificers who are two thieves. It seems that sacrifice and theft are interrelated.

Here, we need to make a clear distinction between Hermes and Prometheus. Hermes, according to Jung, is the archetype of the unconscious.[16] We have learned that one of his main appointments was to act as the messenger of the gods, an appointment inconceivable without the most extreme tolerance. Prometheus is not a god. He is a Titanic figure (though Aeschylus called him a god). "There are many indications that [the name Titan] acquired the connotation of 'wild,' 'rebellious,' or even 'wicked' by opposition to the Olympians…"[17] And the 'unbound' aspect of the

16. *CW* 13, para. 284.
17. Otto, *The Homeric Gods, op. cit.*, p. 33.

Titanic nature, under the guise of Promethean knowledge and technology, has become so predominant in recent historical times that it has become a basic requirement for a cultured analyst to learn how to detect in himself and the patient the Titanic imageless side of human nature and how to deal with it.[18] Camillo saw Prometheus as the carrier of what man does out of necessity and, I would add, for survival. We have to see this drive for survival as having no connection to the instinctual roots of nature; as today's history reveals at a glance, man is more and more alienated from his nature. Prometheus in no way shows the undignified, weakened side of Hermes; on the contrary, he wants to rule the world, but because of the undifferentiated energy of his Titanic nature, it becomes only a power-ridden ambition. He shows only a suspicious and boastful rebellion against the archetypal forms of life, forms he is keen in finding ways to blackmail or destroy. He shows a lack of tolerance, which we feel in the many ways of missionarizing so predominant in today's life, so different from the variety in a Hermes attitude.

Hermes thieves and then sacrifices to the gods all that he has thieved, whereas Prometheus sacrifices to the gods and within that sacrifice he cheats and thieves. If the Hermes sacrifice seems to be the religious sacrifice *par excellence,* then the Prometheus sacrifice is just the opposite – it is openly anti-religious. From this we can assume that the anti-religious function in man is Promethean. We can learn psychologically from these two images of sacrificer and thief, including the cheater, by connecting to them and

18. I have written on the Titanic nature in "Moon Madness – Titanic Love: A Meeting of Pathology and Poetry" in *Images of the Untouched,* eds. Joanne Stroud and Gail Thomas (Pegasus: Dallas, 1982), a theme I am still very involved with in new works in progress. Here, I just touch on it, but it is important to study such a menace to the forms of life, which forces Hermes to compensate today's Promethean challenge by inwardly deepening his nature. For a scholarly study of the Promethean challenge, see E.R. Dodds, *The Ancient Concept of Progress* (Clarendon Press: Oxford, 1973).

animating them within ourselves. Hermes, the mythological cheater, as we shall see later in our reading of the Hymn, is the one who makes the most complete and truly generous sacrifice.

Sacrifice is another important concern of Jung's psychology. In his *Psychological Types*[19] he worked out how sacrifice appeared in two Church Fathers, Origen and Tertullian, in terms of the extraverted and the introverted types. Origen sacrificed his manhood in a concretized external way, whereas Tertullian accepted the internal sacrifice of his intellect. I would like to look again at these two sacrifices, worked out by Jung in connection with the types, from a more archetypal angle. We can see that both Tertullian and Origen were caught from behind by a literalization of religious sacrifice while they were trying to imitate Christ (*imitatio Christi*). To us, today, the sacrifices of Tertullian and Origen seem odd and pathological, devoid of psychization. If, nowadays, we do not see so much of this kind of peculiar sacrifice within the context of religion where, historically, its pathology was contained, we do however see, quite frequently, pathological fantasies of religious sacrifice in both the psychotherapeutical container and in the world political arena, where the appearance of sacrifice has found another container. We see this mixture of religion and politics in the self-immolation of Buddhist monks, the guerilla priests, and the Muslim terrorists.

Jungian psychotherapy pays a great deal of attention to sacrifice, largely based on the psychological functions. A therapeutical movement into the unconscious requires the 'happening' of the sacrifice of the first function, in Jungian terminology referred to as a worn-out persona, old ego attitude, etc. One could say that the process of individuation is reflected through a sequence of sacrifices, experienced mostly in dreams, and verified in the feelings of movement and change in the personality. The approach to sacrifice in

19. C.G. Jung, *Psychological Types*, trans. H.G. Baynes (Routledge & Kegan Paul: London, 1923), p. 19ff.

dreams varies according to the criteria of each Jungian analyst (a spectrum of sacrifice ranging from Hermes to Prometheus). Nevertheless, the classic Jungian concept is based on what is sacrificed as already being worn-out, which gives it a hermetic touch. A routine sacrifice made through the 'will' arouses our suspicion. It is Promethean, in this case for the 'benefit' and health of the soul. Sacrifice is a 'happening'; and from this perspective one can detect the intervention of Hermes, who can guide us along the road of the unconscious and who knows when and how to sacrifice.

One of the main pillars of Jung's work was the connection he made between psychology and religion. All his erudition and experience went into his attempt to delimit the conflict in himself by tracing the invisible borderline where psychology and religion meet. He said again and again that this is as far as we can go with psychology. From here on it is religion. One of Jung's greatest achievements was to contribute to pathology the insights he had gathered from religion. When he was working at 'Burghölzli,' Zurich's university psychiatric clinic, his discovery of connecting the patients' mental delusions to religion was a first and basic contribution in this respect. Undoubtedly this was the first sign that the study of psychology was moving onto *terra firma* and it was the beginning of the study of the archetypes as man's natural and inherited religiosity. We cannot evade his lifetime's work on this conflict in which he sometimes united the borderlines of psychology and religion and at other times demarked them as two separate fields.

In discussing sacrifice, a central element of religion, as told in "The Homeric Hymn to Hermes," it is once more necessary to attempt to insight this borderline. If, for example, we refer the Homeric image of Hermes' sacrifice to that of Abraham, another religious sacrificer, the latter's sacrifice is conceived within the realm of belief. Theft and cheating, so much a part of the imagery we are reading in connection with Hermes, seemingly does not appear. However, we can look at the ritualistic imagery of Abraham's sacrifice and, at the same time, move into that borderline where psychology and religion meet, and thereby include the thieving/cheating side of Hermes without having any intention of destroying the religious context from within which Abraham's religious sacrifice is seen.

In our attempt to delimit this borderline between psychology and religion, we have to apprehend it from the obvious reality that a psychotherapist is not the priest of any religion. Too many psychologists fall into the trap of confusing the two. And, from our insights into this borderline, we need to make a more fluid connection between pathology and religion in psychotherapy. We are aware that a psychology of archetypes deals with elements which, in the history of Western culture, formerly belonged to religion. Many of these religious elements from the base of the standard work of modern psychology, no matter whether it is Freudian or Jungian. Religion lives in us; its forms or the lack of them are reflected in our daily life and, with more precision, the psychotherapist's practice.

After this sacrifice Hermes returned home, slipped back into his cradle and lay playing. Then comes an episode with his mother, who being aware of his activities, castigates him for his misdeeds, whereupon Hermes verifies himself as a thief:

> "Nay, but I will try whatever plan is best, and so feed myself and you continuously. We will not be content to remain here, as you bid, alone of all the gods unfee'd with offerings and prayers. Better to live in fellowship with the deathless gods continually, rich, wealthy, and enjoying stores of grain, than to sit always in a gloomy cave; and, as regards honour, I too will enter upon the rite that Apollo has. If my father will not give it to me, I will seek – and I am able – to be a prince of robbers."

Hermes gives us the image of a god baptizing himself, so to speak, in his own godhood through the affirmation of one of his main attributes – thieving. We do not need to repeat that we center his thieving in the psychic thieving that we have found so essential to Hermes' psychology.

The Hymn goes on to tell how, on the next day, Apollo, aware of the theft of his fifty cows, follows the peculiar tracks left by Hermes and the cows. He arrives at the cave where his brother is lying in his cradle and the two brothers confront each other. Apollo, enraged, asks for his cattle, and Hermes graciously cheats him with these words:

> "Son of Leto, what harsh words are these you have spoken? And is it cattle of the field you are come here to seek? I have not seen them ... Am I like a cattle-lifter, a stalwart person? This is no task for me: rather I care for other things: I care for sleep, and milk of my mother's breast ... and warm baths ... this would be a marvel indeed ... that a child newly born should pass through the forepart of the house with cattle of the field: herein you speak extravagantly. I was born yesterday, and my feet are soft and the ground beneath is rough ... I will swear a great oath ... and vow that neither am I guilty myself, neither have I seen any other who stole your cows – whatever cows may be; for I know them only by hearsay."

With these words to Apollo, another essential characteristic of Hermes makes its appearance. He cheats his brother shamelessly. Before we discuss Hermes' cheating, in order to keep the sequence of the Hymn, we are going to make a small digression into another aspect of Hermes' psychology.

> ... Phoebus Apollo ... took the child and began to carry him. But at that moment the strong Slayer of Argus had his plan, and, while Apollo held him in his hands, sent forth an omen, a hard-worked belly-serf, a rude messenger, and sneezed directly after. And when Apollo heard it, he dropped glorious Hermes out of his hands on the ground:

These somewhat confusing lines describe how Hermes sets about confusing Apollo in order to protect himself. It seems to me that in creating this confusion, Hermes is expressing the omens that belong to his psychology. Perhaps he was teaching Apollo, well-known for his omens, another kind of omen so that Apollo would respect him. We can see that Hermes' omens, manifested in such a corporeal way, bring about in Apollo a complete inability to cope with the situation. No doubt he was thoroughly disgusted. He drops Hermes and the two brothers are now ready for a new movement. I would like to say a bit more about these omens of Hermes, so disgusting to the Apollonian mentality.

Apollo's surprise at his brother's omens gives us a first glimpse into the difference between the two brothers. Apollo is famous for the sacred oracle in his sanctuary at Delphi. The oracle was consulted by the Pythia, a priestess who, seated on a tripod in a state of possession, received the answer sent by the god to the oracular question, an answer in the form of poetical riddles which the priests interpreted. Apollo's oracle needs an external element and gives an answer to a specific question. His oracle was in words, whereas Hermes' omens, manifest in the body, having a physiological, somatic expression, with a feeling and emotional tone. We can risk saying that Hermes' omens have a strange connection with the neuro-vegetative system, expressing themselves with the same autonomy, and are another example of Hermes' connection to deeper strata of human nature, somewhat similar to Burkert's connection of the primitive herma to the animal realm. We have to differentiate this kind of body expression to those of hypochondriac or hysterical manifestations which, while having a strange connection to the body, are repetitive and without a Hermes' insight. Hermes' omens can come in sudden flashes, very like intuitions, in the sense of seeing through, the transparence as Kerényi worked out in his *Hermes: Guide of Souls*,[20] and in their own particular way respond to a given situation, making the body react with an omen. This kind of omen, expressed through the body, can appear in the analyst as an intuition related to the analytical situation he is dealing with.

20. K. Kerényi, *Hermes, Guide of Souls* (Spring Publications: Zurich, 1976), p. 126.

In his seminar on dreams, Jung referred to the omen of the rumbling belly, a noise which is often heard at some distance from the listener, and which brings about what is called an omen in the ensuing dialogue. Many analysts have experienced this kind of hermetic omen and, at its best, it can make a hermetic connection between the psychological events and the body. With his "rude messenger," Hermes shows the trickster side of his nature. It is undoubtedly another very primitive side of the god that is difficult for us to reach in our culture. However, we can catch a hint of its significance in reading Paul Radin's *The Trickster*[21] and also Jung's seminars on Kundalini Yoga where he discussed this 'rude' aspect in the nature of the consciousness of the Mulhadara Chakra and its parallels in Western culture. A more accurate and direct reference to the rumbling belly aspect of the omen is made by E.R. Dodds. In a discussion of *psyche* in Homer he says:

> A man's *thumos* tells him that he must now eat or drink or slay an enemy, it advises him on his course of action, it puts words into his mouth ... He can converse with it, or with his "heart" or his "belly," almost as man to man.[22]

Unfortunately our culture has rather lost touch with sneezing as a hermetic omen. It has become more a medical matter and is mildly and derogatorily called 'a little allergic reaction,' though something of the old attitude remains in the words: 'Bless you,' 'Gesundheit,' and 'Salud.' In *The Origins of European Thought*,[23] Onians refers to the old tradition, in Western culture, of omens through sneezing. A little of this old attitude still lingers in some of the folkloric aspects of our culture, such as in Gallicean magic, in which

21. Paul Radin, *The Trickster* (Schocken Books: New York, 1972).
22. E.R. Dodds, *The Greeks and the Irrational* (University of California Press: Berkeley, 1968), p. 16.
23. Richard Broxton Onians, *The Origins of European Thought* (Cambridge University Press, 1954).

the Meigas, who are probably relics of the old Spanish Celtic priestesses, work their omens through sneezing.

In *The Odyssey*, there is an example of how an omen through sneezing works: When Eumaeus has had the Stranger with him in his cottage for three days and three nights, Penelope summons him to talk with her. He tells her about Odysseus' tales, all his painful adventures, how he was a native of Crete and claimed acquaintance with Odysseus through his family, that he had heard that Odysseus was alive and well and rich. After hearing this Penelope began to talk about the greedy behavior of the Suitors; then she says:

> "The truth is that there is nobody like Odysseus in charge to purge the house of this disease. Ah, if Odysseus could only come back to his own country! He and his son would soon pay them out for their crimes."
>
> As she finished, Telemachus gave a loud sneeze, which echoed round the house in the most alarming fashion. Penelope laughed and turned to Eumaeus. "Do go," she said eagerly, "and bring this stranger here to me. Didn't you notice that my son sneezed a blessing on all I said? That means death, once and for all, to every one of the Suitors: not a man can escape his doom."[24]

There is the interesting psychiatric observation that schizophrenics are unable to sneeze. When they do sneeze, it is a sign of improvement. In connection with this observation, analysts working with psychotic patients have noted that after prolonged psychotherapeutic work they have a bout of sneezing. They consider that this sneezing rids them of psychotic contamination in their work.

After the episode of the omens, there follows a long conversation between the two brothers until the moment when they set off together to put the matter before their

24. Homer, *The Odyssey*, trans. E.V. Rieu (Penguin: Harmondsworth, 1946), Book XVII, p. 273.

father, Zeus. Apollo denounces Hermes and tells the story
of his stolen cattle. Then Hermes answers:

> "Zeus, my father, indeed I will speak truth to you; for I am
> truthful and cannot tell a lie. He came to our house today
> looking for his shambling cows ... He brought no witnesses
> with him nor any of the blessed gods who had seen the theft,
> but with great violence ordered me to confess ... he has the
> rich bloom of glorious youth, while I was born but yesterday ...
> Believe my tale ... that I did not drive his cows to my house ...
> nor crossed the threshold: this I say truly ... You yourself know
> that I am not guilty: and I will swear a great oath upon it ... And
> some day I will punish him, strong as he is, for this pitiless
> inquisition; but now do you help the younger."
>
> So spake the Cyllenian, the Slayer of Argus, while he kept
> shooting sidelong glances and kept his swaddling clothes upon
> his arm, and did not cast them away. But Zeus laughed out loud
> to see his evil-plotting child well and cunningly denying guilt
> about the cattle.

Here we have arrived at the appropriate imagery to
discuss cheating as seen from its archetypal roots. Cheating
belongs to a god. All the gods are important, but the god of
cheaters and cheating is particularly crucial in the legacy of
Jungian psychology. Jung wrote a great deal about Hermes/
Mercury, so he is of capital importance in his psychology.

Throughout our discussion of cheating, I want to keep
very close to the imagery of Hermes first cheating his
brother and then cheating his father. We should not move
into those worn-out notions of a society that demands the
truth, the whole truth, and nothing but the truth, notions
coming from other archetypal traditions in Western culture.
It is only by connecting to the imagery – Hermes cheating
his brother, Apollo, and his father, Zeus – that we can gain
any profitable idea about cheating. Hermes showed an art
and shamelessness in his cheating, both facets being very
much part of his nature. I would like to read this scene of a
father with his two sons as accurately as possible. By responding with a laugh to his son Hermes' barefaced cheating,

Zeus has accepted his son's nature and life-style. We don't know how Apollo reacted, but we can guess that, his archetypal configuration being the exact opposite of Hermes, he was outraged at a cheating expressed so naturally. Apollo is interested in detecting falsehood and searching for the truth; he is the god of moderation, a quality his brother does not show in his cheating. Apollo rules ritual cleanliness, both in its religious purificatory aspect and in the sense of manners. We have seen how that rude rumbling belly of Hermes was incomprehensible to him. Apollo rules the academic world, its brilliance and rational order; we can say he is behind what we call success in society , elements which Hermes can acknowledge but never identify with.

Zeus is the Rainmaker, the *pater familias,* the ruling principle, the balancer of the personality. He alone carries the principle of monotheism as far as the Greeks conceived it,[25] but, above all, he is the principle of tolerance in Greek polytheism: he has respect and tolerance for the individualities and different natures of his brothers and sisters, his sons and daughters. Zeus centered the Greek religion and way of life. He and his son Apollo belong to the archetypal carriers of collective consciousness, to the establishment. One of Apollo's surnames was "the consciousness of Zeus," meaning the son acted as a mirror in which the father reflected certain aspects of life outside his own consciousness. Let us take as an example a father who is a businessman or has a professional career, whose son follows successfully in his father's path. The father nourishes his own consciousness and prevents its petrification through his interest in the studies and activities of the son. The son reflects the spirit of the epoch and the generation gap is bridged. A variant of this scene of Zeus with his two sons appears in the alchemical treatise "The Book of Lambspring."[26] Zeus and Apollo appear as the King and the

25. Martin P. Nilsson, *History of Greek Religion,* trans. F.J. Fielden (W.W. Norton: New York, 1964) is recommended for those readers interested.

Prince, under the symbolism of the old worn-out, sick, and rigid King and the Prince with new ideas. It is Hermes who makes the bridge between them, bringing a reconciliation of the old and the new at a higher level. So we can see that this meeting between Zeus and his two sons is in itself archetypal, offering psychological movement and a widening of consciousness.

Zeus is also the principle of authority, and I would like the reader to keep this scene as a mirror in which to reflect the episode between Freud and Jung we discussed in the last chapter.

Hermes, as we have said before following Jung, is the archetype of the unconscious, and he is also a cheater. He is the god who propitiates psychic movement, therefore we can postulate too that his cheating belongs to the complexities of psychic movement. Hermes, Otto writes: "… is the spirit of a constellation which recurs in most diverse conditions and which embraces loss as well as gain, mischief as well as kindliness. Though much of this must seem questionable from a moral point of view, nevertheless it is a configuration which belongs to the fundamental aspects of living reality…"[27] And we can add cheating to loss and gain, mischief and kindliness. Hermes introduces himself as a cheater accepting such a reality, a reality very different from that of his brother Apollo. If we take their dialogue and convey it into modern psychological terms, we can see it as a dialogue between the collective consciousness or superego and the unconscious. The gracefulness of the old Hymn enables us to catch a glimpse into these two sides of the psyche long before they appeared as the tremendous split they became in Western culture. The conflict between ruling consciousness (equivalent to Zeus and Apollo) and the unconscious (equivalent to Hermes) is well known as being at the core of psychotherapy. The Hymn gives us a

26. Arthur Edward Waite, *The Hermetic Museum* (Robinson & Watkins, 1973), Vol. I.
27. Otto, *The Homeric Gods, op. cit.,* p. 122.

lesson in how these two psychic forces can come together again without any uniting symbol: these two gods, these two forces, accept each other's reality, each other's differences, and yet go on talking, bartering, and cheating.

The ruling principles, Zeus and Apollo, even if they do not cheat in the barefaced manner of Hermes, do lie when the spirit they represent is no longer valid historically. When the statement they are holding onto is no longer valid, or when the premise they are using has nothing to do with the person to whom they are addressing it, then their statement or promise becomes false. However the main interest of this part of the Hymn would be to keep it as a model of a younger son cheating his older brother and father, thereby making a very psychological connection and introducing them to a very alien way of being: the psychology of cheating. The secret of this kind of cheating is that it is hermetic. Hermes would never fall into the trap of talking with his elder brother and father from the viewpoint of the ruling consciousness they represent.

Many analysts have seen a paralyzed psyche or a life destroyed because a son has been unable to respond to the parental demand of going in for an orderly academic career, of being a brilliant success in the Apollonic world of today. And there are those cases where the son is unable to express his own nature because it belongs to an archetype other than the one imposed by the parental demand and society. Today's ruling consciousness is so Apollonic that what falls outside it is outcast. The son is unable to express his nature in an acceptable way, as Hermes does in the Hymn, i.e., cheating, a hermetic cheating which would protect his psyche, move it, and relativize the parental image.

Hermes' cheating of his older brother and father should be taken into consideration for psychotherapy, for it opens a wider commerce with his brother as we shall see later in the Hymn. At the level of family psychology, this scene gives us the chance to see cheating as another way of connecting to the home divinities. Hermes connects in many ways. We can add his cheating of Apollo and Zeus to the way he connected to his father and mother on the day he was born, that first song. Both belong to the same complex and attitude. In our study of this god we will see that he uses these ways of connecting more than once.

In psychotherapy, when the analyst claims to be only the analyst and the patient is only the patient, there is an element of falsehood in the situation. The analyst who demands the truth and nothing but the truth is possibly more in the role of the religious confessor, with some characteristics of the inquisitor, than a believer in a psychotherapy backed by Hermes' imagery. Such an attitude creates an asymmetry in the archetypal situation, i.e., the analyst knowing the 'truth' and expecting the analysand to tell that 'truth.' Here we do not see Hermes' symmetry in which cheating is lived in the hermetic sense as a propitious vehicle for making the connection and for moving the psyche.

After listening to his two sons, Zeus puts things in order. He bids Hermes and Apollo to be of one mind and search out the cattle. It is as if he were telling his two sons to get to know each other, to learn more about each other's nature. For our study of the archetypes, which is based on recognizing the differences in archetypal patterns of the gods and goddesses, this getting to know each other seems to be the most useful way of looking at this part of the story. Zeus confirms this order by bowing his head (*numinosum*).

The two brothers, Hermes leading the way, go to the river Alpheus where Hermes had left the cattle:

> Now while Hermes went to the cave in the rock and began to drive out the strong cattle, the son of Leto, looking aside, saw the cowhides on the sheer rock. And he asked glorious Hermes at once:
>
> "How were you able, you crafty rogue, to flay two cows, newborn and babyish as you are? For my part I dread the strength that will be yours: there is no need you should keep growing long, Cyllenian son of Maia!"

> So saying Apollo twisted strong withes with his hands mean-
> ing to bind Hermes with firm bands; but the bands would not
> hold him and the withes of osier fell far from him and began to
> grow at once from the ground beneath their feet... And
> intertwining with one another, they quickly grew and covered
> all the wild-roving cattle by the will of the thievish Hermes, so
> that Apollo was astonished and gazed.

With this episode we are probably facing the essential
difference between the two brothers. Apollo tries to control
Hermes' movements. Evidently he is afraid of something
alien and beyond his understanding in Hermes' ability to
slay two cows on the day of his birth. Hermes, in keeping
with his nature, slips out of his brother's grasp. The image
could be said to convey that elusive quality of Hermes, the
impossibility of ever catching him, which, during the Middle
Ages, was seen symbolically in the alchemical quicksilver.
There is another important aspect to this image, because it
suggests that Hermes cannot be bound by any other form,
that the conventional forms of Apollo – brilliant ideas,
refined conceptual speech, the honor of the academy, etc. –
do not bind Hermes.

In his practice, a psychotherapist has to deal almost daily
with the conflictive aspect of this image, either in terms of
the already mentioned son whose nature is unable to
respond to the parental demand or in terms of the more
dramatic therapeutical task of trying to hermetically unbind
the patient whose main problem is too strong an affiliation
to the Apollonic world. Apollo centers modern man's consciousness, and we are aware of the danger and pathology in
this onesidedness. It takes a great deal of hermetic art and
patience to unbind a person from an Apollonic rigidity,
which, though backed by success in life and society, is
usually accompanied with deep unease, meaninglessness,
depression, histrionic hysteria, and psychosomatic complaints. The unbinding has to be kept within the limits of
hermetic psychic life, because this sort of patient is full of
fear, equating unbinding with chaos.

To beguile Apollo, Hermes took the lyre and began to play and sing:

And Phoebus Apollo laughed for joy; for the sweet throb of the marvellous music went to his heart, and a soft longing took hold on his soul as he listened ... seized with a longing not to be allayed, and he opened his mouth and spoke winged words to Hermes:

"Slayer of oxen, trickster, busy one, comrade of the feast, this song of yours is worth fifty cows, and I believe that presently we shall settle our quarrel peacefully. But come now, tell me this, resourceful son of Maia: Has this marvellous thing been with you from your birth, or did some god or mortal man give it to you...? [Evidently, it is difficult for Apollo to see what man does by nature.] For wonderful is this new-uttered sound I hear... What skill is this? What song for desperate cares? What way of song? For verily here are three things to hand all at once from which to choose, – mirth, and love, and sweet sleep... I am filled with wonder, O son of Zeus, at your sweet playing."

Then Hermes answered him in artful words: "You question me carefully, O Far-worker; yet I am not jealous that you should enter upon my art: this day you shall know it. For I seek to be friendly with you both in thought and word. Now you well know all things in your heart, since you sit foremost among the deathless gods ... and are goodly and strong. And wise Zeus loves you as all right is, and has given you splendid gifts... Now you are free to learn whatever you please; but since, it seems, your heart is so strongly set on playing the lyre, chant, and play upon it, giving yourself to merriment, taking this as a gift from me, and do you, my friend, bestow glory on me... I will give this lyre, glorious son of Zeus, while I for my part will graze down with the wild-roving cattle the pastures on the hill and horse-feeding plain; so shall the cows covered by the bulls calve abundantly, both males and females. And now there is no need for you, bargainer though you are, to be furiously angry."

When Hermes had said this, he held out the lyre: and Phoebus Apollo took it, and readily put his shining whip in Hermes' hand, and ordained him keeper of the herds. The son of Maia received it joyfully, while ... the lord far-working

> Apollo, took the lyre ... and tried each string with the key.
> Awesomely it sounded at the touch of the god...

Hermes' playing on the lyre enchants Apollo and the ice is broken. The two brothers begin to bargain. In giving his lyre to Apollo, Hermes' generosity brings about a reciprocity in Apollo, and he is no longer so set on getting back his cattle.

When Hermes says: "I am not jealous that you should enter upon my art: this day shall you know it. For I seek to be friendly with you in both thought and word," there is a more subtle and deep expression of his nature. He accepts Apollo's covetousness, has no need to regard his music jealously, and is ready to be friendly to him: He is not concerned with whether or not Apollo's nature is alien to his. He expresses his generosity without jealousy, and friendliness is fundamental to his nature. As Otto stresses, Hermes is the friendliest of the gods.[28]

Peter Walcott, in his book *Envy and the Greeks*[29] discusses how in classical and Christian literature the words envy and jealousy are interchangeable, though they mean two different things. The jealousy mentioned above in the context of the Hymn has the connotation of envy – envy of attributes and inventiveness. Hermes is telling his brother that he is not envious of anything Apollo could do with the lyre he has invented, a point worthy of note and reflection; he is not going to be envious of Apollo's success as a patron of music. But one feels that Apollo would tend to be envious of another person's ideas and skills. Envy is involved in the relationships between two persons of the same sex, whereas jealousy (as we shall discuss in Chapter III) has a sexual connotation and implies three people, one of whom is, generally speaking, of the opposite sex. Hermes says very clearly that envy is not part of his nature.

---

28. *Ibid.*, p. 107.
29. (Aris & Phillips: Warminster, 1978), Chapter 1, "Introduction."

Here, I would like to write a few lines about envy. In Jungian studies, envy has been discussed mostly in connection with fairy tales – the motif of two elder sisters' envy for the younger (Cinderella, Eros and Psyche, etc.), and there is the tendency to resolve envy at the easy fairy-tale-level of the destruction of the two sisters, with this, implying there is a new consciousness of envy. It is considered a shadow business of which one has to be conscious. However the Jungians of the first generation were aware of its psychosomatic implications, above all Miss Barbara Hannah, who, in her lectures, discussed the evil eye as a physical expression of envy. We can be sure that Hermes, with his connection to his psychosomatic nature, would very quickly detect any peculiar physical expression of envy.

Reading Walcott, one realizes that, in the Greek culture, envy was not a capital sin as in Christianity; instead there was an awareness of its complexities and implications. Ostracism was the penalty for someone who caused too much envy. This shows how conscious they must have been of it. One can imagine Hermes vanishing whenever envy is constellated; he sees its evil aspect as did the Greeks. Envy is included in W.B. Stanford's catalogue of emotions in his *Greek Tragedy and the Emotions,* but evidently no envious character appears in Greek tragedy; it was considered too villainous and therefore unsuitable.[30]

As regards the musical aspect of this part of the Hymn, I have had several musicians in psychotherapy, all of them Apollonic, showing what is probably an Apollonic pathology in that their conception of music was based solely on discipline and techniques leading to perfection, all obvious Apollonic ingredients. They brought a picture of a guilt neurosis which was projected upon the rules of discipline, technique and perfection, their psychology being mostly ruled by the *puer aeternus,* success and brilliance, with a lot of hysterical moodiness, criticism, and eventual psychop-

30. W.B. Stanford, *Greek Tragedy and the Emotions* (Routledge & Kegan Paul: London, 1983), p. 35.

athy. They lived and played their music from the Apollonic side only, completely neglecting the body, the psychic body, which could hold and contain both themselves and their playing. The conception behind my attitude to the psychotherapy of these patients was to propitiate a movement from Apollo back to Hermes: to let Hermes pick up his lyre again and play it, that hermetic playing of the lyre, so lacking in the musical conception of Western man, whose music is mostly caught up in the cerebral romantic sentiments of Apollo.

But let us return to the shining whip, the attribute or symbol of the shepherd. The symbolism of the shepherd is an important motif in Western culture. This attribute, offered to Hermes by Apollo as part of an interchange, has become symbolized and has the connotation of a leader leading his followers. Of Hermes, Otto also says: "Hermes is the kindliest spirit who leads the flocks from their folds in the morning and faithfully guides them on their way..." However, he adds: "But here too this kindly service is only one side of his activity. The guide can also lead astray."[31]

Just as the symbolism of the shepherd has been fundamental in Western culture, so too it appears in the study of Psychology, where the leaders of the different schools 'shepherd' their followers. And this metaphor of the shepherd is not without some foundation. We are indebted to these leaders and founders of psychology. They opened the door into psychology itself and passed on to us their discoveries, knowledge and experience. We have seen followers of a particular school who have profited greatly from the guidance of the leader. But we can also see that, though benefitting from that guidance in many ways, they have, in other ways, been led astray. This could be due to a tendency to absolutize the guidance of the master, to make a sort of theology out of the master's teaching. Absolutizing has nothing to do with Hermes. These followers have not kept within the constancy of the archetype – guiding the way and

31. Otto, *The Homeric Gods, op. cit.,* p. 110.

leading astray – the double axis of the outer and inner shepherd.

The basic knowledge the analyst acquires from the history of psychology and his school is one thing, and the way he thieves hermetically from a relevant figure in the field, his patients, and the world he lives in, is another. The predominant attitude in twentieth-century psychology is that of the followers of the school practising psychotherapy by way of dogmas made out of the knowledge acquired and living, psychotherapeutically speaking, a life in a sect. This is far from an attitude that propitiates the nourishment of the psyche through the many possibilities life offers; on the contrary, life's events are reduced and labeled with the knowledge provided by the school.

After this initial exchange, the two brothers returned to "snowy Olympus delighting in the lyre. Then wise Zeus was glad and made them both friends." It would seem to be under the convivial influence of Zeus that "Hermes loved the son of Leto continually." In the meantime Hermes managed to invent another musical instrument: "the pipes whose sound is heard afar." With an act of creation, does giving away that creation make further creation possible? In the earlier discussion of sacrifice, it was shown that the proper sacrifice enables energy to move in a rotation (the alchemical *rotatio*) and petrification is avoided. Thus, in the same way, by giving away the creation, there is the possibility of more energy for more creation. It would seem that this movement of the libido only happens within the archetypal sphere of Hermes.

There is something of a contradiction in that the master of thieves is not at all jealous (envious) when his brother seeks to thieve his art. Hermes' friendliness and generosity are very moving if we consider that they are a peculiarity of the god who is supposed to be the cheater and thief *par excellence*. It is another facet of his nature that we can add to his sacrificing to the gods in the most honorable way, though he is the greatest of all thieves and cheaters.

Hermes gives his lyre to Apollo and Apollo reciprocates by giving Hermes his shining whip and ordaining him "Keeper of the Herds." It is as if, with this bartering, a recognition of each other's nature begins to appear. Could this exchange between two men of very different natures be what moves them into love, into eros among men, by way of a primordial bartering? Apollo's gift of the shining whip and his making Hermes the Keeper of Herds could be seen as an expression of eros among men. It might very well belong to the archetypal background of chivalry: a friendly recognition of each other's qualities without envy. Later on in this study, when we come to the story of Hermes and Dryops, we shall discuss eros among men from another archetypal background. With this present image, we have a new perspective from which we might have a conception of what underlines the word 'magnanimity.' Magnanimity could be conceived as recognition without pettiness. This imagery of bartering, this easy commerce between the gods, can be suggestive for a psychotherapy that would accept bartering as a way to connect and move psyche, as another way to connect these two archetypes that have been so separated in our culture, resulting in conflict and pathology.

Historically, the main opposition between two psychic structures (two gods with their archetypal patterns) has been maintained by the opposition between Apollo and Dionysus. From Orpheus to Nietzsche to Jung, we know that the attempt to bring together such opposed natures means: in the case of Orpheus, a myth of destruction; in the case of Nietzsche, an ingredient of his madness; in the case of Jung, an insight into where destruction and madness can occur. Jung realized that in diagnosing the conflict of these two opposite natures in man, one is diagnosing a pathology in depth. In his conception of the psychological types, based on the opposed natures in man (the opposites), he discussed the two I have just mentioned: Apollo and Dionysus; and the introduction of this conception into psychotherapy was probably an attempt to reconcile these two opposed natures; though Jung's ideas moved in another direction –

the reconciliation of the opposites, wholeness, etc. But these two opposites, Apollo and Dionysus, could find a model in the relationship between Apollo and Hermes in the Hymn that would offer a middle way, that could propitiate psychological movement. Then the whole idea of reconciling the opposites, which in psychotherapy has usually meant moving the Apollonic onesidedness into the most repressed realm of the psyche, where Dionysus is, would be unnecessary, and, in any event, would only be possible through Hermes guiding the psyche.

We have been discussing two ways of reconciling these two archetypes – by cheating and bartering. Our next passage in the Hymn offers further reflections upon ways of connection:

> "Son of Maia, guide and cunning one, I fear you may steal from me the lyre and my curved bow together; for you have an office from Zeus, to establish deeds of barter amongst men throughout the fruitful earth. Now if you would only swear me the great oath of the gods, either by nodding your head, or by the potent waters of Styx, you would do all that can please and ease my heart."
>
> Then Maia's son nodded his head and promised that he would never steal anything of all the Far-shooter possessed, and would never go near his strong house.
>
> … But Apollo, son of Leto, swore to be fellow and friend to Hermes, vowing that he would love no other among the immortals, neither god nor man sprung from Zeus, better than Hermes: and the Father sent forth an eagle in confirmation.

The picture deepens. First, it conveys again the difference between the two brothers. Apollo is paranoiac and afraid of being stolen from by Hermes. Yet, at the same time, he brings about in the narrative that Hermes has "an office from Zeus to establish deeds of barter amongst men…" In this image, we find a meeting ground in the human soul for the paranoid fear of being robbed and the office given to Hermes for commerce on earth. It is an important image from which to insight either the opposition or the meeting of the two brothers in us.

Historians tell us about the antagonism between commerce a despotic ruling power. The relationship between the ruling center of a kingdom and the frontiers of that kingdom, where commerce took place, can give us, on the one hand, an archetypal image and, on the other, historical evidence of what is going on in that kingdom. The historians relate that when the relationship between the central power (the King) and the merchants is fluent and cooperative, the kingdom is prosperous; but when the ruling power becomes despotic, antagonism and serious conflict develop between the ruling power and trade, and the prosperity of the kingdom stagnates. The historical image shows a psychological condition which Jung dealt with, symbolizing it beautifully in his alchemical interpretations. The despotism, the rigidity of the King, probably has to do with his fear of being robbed, fear springing from the unconscious which defies any attempt to rationalize it. Throughout history despotism has blocked commerce, and what is valid in the historical economy is also valid for the psyche. The historical image is similar to the image we have of some patients with whom we can see no possibility of trading; there is no meeting; the center is despotic and thus excludes the flexibility needed for any commerce. This exclusion of commerce would seem to stem from an overwhelming fear. We cannot see Hermes as god of commerce in these patients.

To put this in terms of the therapeutic metaphor: when Hermes as god of commerce does appear in a case of severe rigidity, we begin to see an improvement in the patient. When the image of Hermes as god of commerce is not repressed, he procures relationship among men, the discovery of the world, and the potpourri we are living in today. Hermes propitiates trade, interchange, and survival in both history and psyche. Throughout history, trading has been one of the ways of natural survival, and it is one of the ways in which two conflicting archetypal patterns can meet.

There are times when we all have a fear of being robbed or cheated, and with this fear comes despotism (power). We have to realize that, when this despotism appears, with its paranoiac and psychopathic aspect, there is no room for Hermes to trade, no room for a meeting between these two opposite natures in our soul. Likewise in psychotherapy, if the fear is not accepted when the thieving, cheating aspect of Hermes appears, then the analytical situation is in danger of moving into despotic power and the psyche stagnates. The situation becomes asymmetric.

In the analyst/patient relationship, there is a worn-out denominator of 'understanding.' Far back in 1912,[32] Jung viewed the longing for understanding as a longing for the mother and as a regression into the mother complex. Again and again, understanding is sought after as the basis of the therapeutic situation. There are psychotherapists who think a real psychotherapy means to know what is the cause at the core of the patient's illness; then all the analytical activity is aimed at this goal. This is not only a frightening conception but a pretentious one and alarming to a hermetic conscious-ness which would feel its psychic movement threatened, by being substituted by a monstrous personality. "The Homeric Hymn to Hermes" offers a wider scope by showing us two gods, behind two different archetypal structures in the psyche, who deal with each other in a psychology of barter and exchange. Their bartering suggests another model for psychotherapy. One does not need to 'know' or have a deep understanding of the other, for there is a psychology of bartering which, in itself, is therapeutic. The most wide-spread Jungian psychotherapeutic concern is to move the onesidedness of the personality which is too caught in the luminosity of Apollo; and this scene of bartering is sugges-tive for what would be a minimal therapeutic request: to encourage that polarized consciousness to become acquainted with its opposite.

32. *CW* 5, para. 682.

The relationship between the two brothers improves substantially when Hermes promises that "he would never steal anything of all the Far-shooter possessed and would never go near his strong house." With this promise, there is a delineation of their two fields which, of course, soothes Apollo and he is ready to love Hermes above all others. The defining of the limits of their two fields of action, the marking of the boundaries, brings about a movement into love, eros, between the two brothers. A true distance has been created. Hermes shows that he is able to make a differentiation, that this ability is not just Apollonian. This marking of the boundaries between two archetypal figures gives us another image from which to reflect eros among men.

> And Apollo swore also: "Verily I will make you only to be an omen for the immortals and all alike, trusted and honoured by my heart. Moreover, I will give you a splendid staff of riches and wealth: it is of gold, with three branches and will keep you scatheless, accomplishing every task, whether of words or deeds that are good, which I claim to know through the utterance of Zeus. But as for soothsaying, noble, heaven-born child, of which you ask, it is not lawful for you to learn it, nor for any other of the deathless gods: only the mind of Zeus knows that. I am pledged and have vowed and sworn a strong oath that no other of the eternal gods save I should know the wise-hearted counsel of Zeus. And do not you, my brother, bearer of the golden wand, bid me tell those decrees which all-seeing Zeus intends...
>
> But I will tell you another thing, Son of all-glorious Maia and Zeus who holds the aegis, luck-bringing genius of the gods. There are certain holy ones, sisters born – three virgins gifted with wings: their heads are besprinkled with white meal, and they dwell under a ridge of Parnassus. These are teachers of divination apart from me... From their home they fly now here, now there, feeding on honey-comb and bringing all things to pass. And when they are inspired through eating yellow honey, they are willing to speak truth; but if they be deprived of the god's sweet food, then they speak falsely, as

they swarm in and out together. These, then, I give you; enquire of them strictly and delight your heart: and if you should teach any mortal so to do, often will he hear your response – if he have good fortune."

Apollo, accomplishing Zeus' will, makes Hermes "only to be an omen for the immortals and all alike." The image seems to say that Hermes himself is an omen. An omen gives us a feeling of prognosis, or foreboding; it is a foreshadowing. We receive a warning that connects us to our nature, and which is always within the limitations of our own history.

The most extreme feeling would be a sort of presage born of natural means: the realm of Hermes, what happens in man's nature. This sort of omen could be said to manifest from Hermes' connection with the natural man's basic instinct for survival. We can imagine a man travelling along the obscure roads of life, either guided or led astray by Hermes, and in need of an instinctual omen to mark his movement along the road. This kind of omen, or guidance, both connects man to his nature and comes out of his nature at the necessary moment for survival. When Hermes appears in dreams and fantasies he can be taken as an omen, either guiding the psychotherapy or conveying the prognosis contained in the omen.

In any case, Hermes, or any of his attributes, appearing in fantasies or dreams is a sign that psychic movement is constellated, opening the way to Hermes' possibilities in psychotherapy. I had as a case a physician in his fifties, whose onesidedness was very rigid. He used to come and see me from time to time, full of distance and suspicion towards psychotherapy. Eventually he brought me the common dream of feeling there were people in the garden of his house. He came down the stairs with a gun just as a thief was opening the door, whereupon he fired all the bullets out of his gun, killing the thief. He was delighted with his action in the dream and afterwards in his conscious attitude, in spite of all my attempts to reflect this destructive and repressive attitude towards a part of himself. He disappeared and a few years later I heard that he had had a serious heart attack. I leave the reader to his or her own speculations.

Earlier, we discussed the preliminary aspects of the omen side of Hermes manifesting in physical reactions. Now the narrative describes the true epiphany of Hermes as an omen in himself. What before was very difficult for Apollo to bear is now totally accepted. It is further delimiting of the two brothers' fields of action, each one's territory, and it demonstrates an ever increasing acceptance.

Then Apollo says: "Moreover, I will give you a splendid staff." Hermes' staff, or wand, has been seen as his magical side. This staff became, later, a symbol of the medical profession, thus connecting Hermes to the complexities of the healing archetype and so to Asclepius. The intimacy of his connection to Asclepius was seen in Hellenistic times and was expressed in hermetic literature. The omens of Hermes, which we discussed before in regard to the body, now include the new attribute of the wand that, by its touch, accomplishes every task and brings a touch of magic.

The notions of magic, the magical realm of the psyche and the magical expectations of curing and healing provided by anthropology, have not varied very much from primitive to modern man. Modern man, as we all know, is full of awed magical expectation waiting for the latest pill or laser rays that will cure him. This sort of magical expectation at its most stupid and foolish peaked a few years ago when the scientific world thought of atomic energy as a healing panacea, when in reality we are cringing before its terrible destructive potential. Magical expectations accompany each person who goes into psychotherapy, regardless of his intellectual status, age, or the conflicts he is suffering. Jungian psychology has paid some attention to the magical side of healing, discussing fairy tales, where the magic wand appears, and the shamanistic cures in anthropological material; also detecting its presence in psychotherapy in those sudden deep awarenesses which seem to be magical in their suddenness.

There has been some concern with how therapists can become identified with magical elements of the archetype, with the magical power of healing, and so psychotherapeutic practice becomes pervaded by magical expectations. It is here that the charlatan enters psychotherapy with his magical slogans, such as, psychotherapy is a way to individuation, or that it is a clean, pure activity, while denying the archetypal complexities clustered around the word magic. I use the word 'slogan' in this context because it expresses the outer collective's attraction to magic healing. But you cannot make a slogan of Jung's inferior function or Ziegler's ideas concerning the recessive traits in man's nature.[33] As far as we can move them, the complexities of magic healing have a connection to the archetype of healing but have been discussed mostly in relation to power due to the practitioners' unconscious identification with this aspect of the archetype. Sometimes a state of 'possession' is experienced. I would say possession is one way the archetype functions. I cannot, for example, conceive the energy of surgeons, operating night and day for hours without feeling any exhaustion even at an age when physical capacity tends to diminish, in any other terms than that of possession. To repeat, power has been seen in relation to identification with the archetype and this identification breaks the archetype of healing and it no longer functions; or, to put it in the language of Hermes: Hermes disappears from the scene. The therapist is left fighting, with all the strength of his power, against the illness of the patient, who becomes a puppet feeding the power of such a merciless practitioner. This power, stemming from an identification with the archetype, could be accepted as not being so terribly derogatory in itself. Without being cynical, we can say that in the healing adventure between patient and therapist, there are two histories, two fates, meeting in time. It is a synchronistic event, neither good nor bad, a destiny, and must be

---

33. Alfred Ziegler, *Archetypal Medicine, op. cit.,* "Theoria" (Spring Publications: Dallas, 1983).

included in whatever we call healing. Wherever we stand in regard to healing, whether in terms of an emergency or an adventure in depth, it is a chance encounter between therapist and patient, and we sense Hermes' presence, expressing himself as lord of the roads, guiding our psyche and body, or leading astray.

Power, in respect to healing, has been discussed in terms of a split archetype: magic power as an attempt to deal with the broken archetype of healing; but no healing can come out of an archetype that is broken. I personally am not interested in discussing the idea of the split archetype. Perhaps it throws some light on power and also enables us to see more clearly a madness taking over the relationship between practitioner and patient. However, as far as I am concerned, where power comes into healing, the archetype simply does not function and Hermes, the connection-maker, vanishes.

In reality, we know very little about power in itself, and it is difficult for us to accept that it is deeply ingrained in human nature, using and manipulating the forms of life, the archetypes. Power is the biggest challenge to the studies of psychology, because all the knowledge acquired by the so-called healing profession can be turned into superficial notions to be used by a power-ridden practitioner just for the sake of power.

My own approach to the image of Hermes as magician was stimulated by the work of the modern scholars who offer a new perspective and a reflection of how the spirit of our time wants to re-apprehend what underlies the word 'magic.' Rather than lean on anthropological studies, fairy tales and shamanism, I prefer to turn to Frances Yates. She writes:

> ... the view of Bruno's memory systems as magical ancestors of the mind machine is only partially valuable and must not be pressed too far. If we drop the word 'magical' and think of the efforts of an occult memory artist as directed towards drawing out of the psyche combinations of 'archetypal' images we come

within the range of some major trends of modern psychological thought. However, as with the mind machine analogy, I would not stress a Jungian analogy which might confuse more than it illuminates.[34]

Let us imitate Miss Yates and drop the word 'magical' and think in terms of those psychic combinations of archetypal images – the combinations the patients bring and those arising in the analytical situation – which the psychotherapist has learned and which form his psychotherapeutical memory. The Jungian analogy that Miss Yates evades depends on the line of Jungian thought one is following: whether that of phylogenetic amplification, fairy tales, shamanism, etc., "which might confuse" or drive us into the identification and power we have already discussed, or that of an archetypal approach where the combination of archetypal images provides the field where reflection can happen and Hermes appear.

The image of Hermes with his magic wand, making one of his epiphanies, needs to be gathered into a psychotherapy based on the archetypes. Hermes was a follower of Mnemosyne (Memory) and he is the connection-maker. These two aspects of Hermes can combine with the archetypal images that underlie the word 'magic' and contain them within the memory system of the psychotherapeutic process, not as something seemingly magic, but well-rooted in a memory which can procure psychic movement. This combination of Hermes and Mnemosyne, seen as a soul memory with its emotional component, is what makes possible the art of psychotherapy and analogical thinking. We know that analogies complement reflection and are what most move the psyche.[35]

When Apollo tells Hermes that it is not lawful for him to learn soothsaying, the Hymn seems to say implicitly that soothsaying is not Hermes' business, though, as we know, he does receive a kind of divination. 'Sooth' means truth, and,

34. Yates, *The Art of Memory, op. cit.,* p. 252.

as the Hymn shows, we cannot talk much about truth to
Hermes. Soothsaying, divination, and oracles are elements
that belong to the realm of Zeus and Apollo.[36] These
phenomena appeared in Greece during a time when there
was a historical necessity for all the possibilities of the
psyche. It is difficult to conceive of a psychotherapy of
soothsaying, though it seems there are psyches that only
find a certain balance by way of constantly relating psychotherapeutic material, dreams, and fantasies to foretelling or
predicting the future. And let us not forget that this component is in everybody; it is archetypal.

However, Hermes does receive an odd kind of divination
by way of the three weird, virginal sisters who seem to be bee-
like creatures. Their image gives us an impression of how
the virginal side of the psyche appears in Hermes. Could it
be how Hermes connects to the Artemis/Diana virginal
element with its own Luna time, a connection through these
three sisters appearing here and there, telling truth or falsity
according to the amount of honey received? We can insight
that with this kind of divination, truth and falsity and the
experience of them as opposites, disappear. From all we
have learned about Hermes so far, he is not concerned with
what is true or what is false.

A patient can enter into psychotherapy with a strong
constellation of this kind of divination (a strong, virginal,
hebephrenic component), who tends to give honey, only
honey, to the analyst. In this case the three virgins can be a
recourse, in that there is a 'honied' psychotherapy in which
truth or falsity is not the point. For as long as the analyst is
aware of the constellation, he can approach the patient

35. To reflect through analogies and the art of rhetoric is at the base of
Western culture: in *The Iliad,* when Agamemnon sent his three ambas-
sadors – Odysseus, Phoenix, and Ajax – to apologize to Achilles and
persuade him to return to the fight, it was Phoenix who moved him the
most by bringing the analogy of Meleager. See George A. Kennedy,
*Classical Rhetoric and its Christian and Secular Tradition from Ancient to
Modern Times* (Croom Helm: London, 1980), pp. 11-15.
36. H.W. Parke, *Greek Oracles* (Hutchinson: London, 1967).

from within the constellation and procure the happening of psychotherapy. But if the analyst is not aware, then no psychotherapy is possible and the virginal lunatic time of the patient is merely increased.

It becomes evident from our reading of this passage in the Hymn that there is something of an archetypal mixture in divination. It is an attribute shared by the brothers, though each has his own style. Depending on the analyst's acute awareness of which archetype may be dominating the situation, a lot can be rescued for psychotherapy. As our concern is the practical side of psychotherapy, we have to try to introduce some differentiation into the elements of divination. Divination and soothsaying happen in psycho-therapy in both apollonic and hermetic ways. Dream inter-pretation or a discussion can be conducted from the apol-lonic side of divination. The analyst's archetypal connection to Apollo, giving a brilliant, practical, and scientific touch, moves the situation towards the oracular needs of the psyche. Or the response can come from the Hermes side of divination. The three virginal sisters, appearing within the Hermes complex, guide the divinatory constellation accord-ing to the honey the patient brings to the analyst. He, if unconscious of the virgins' divination in himself, demands more and more honey in order to give back more divina-tion. He can become unconscious of a situation that has at the very least a hebephrenic touch; but if he is aware of this virginal honey in the psychotherapy, then, in spite of its apparent childishness, Hermes is there.

From this sharing of divination between Apollo and Hermes, we can speculate that if, in the middle of a transfer-ential process guided by Hermes, with all the associated complexes, an enigma arises which seeks to be resolved by way of divination, there must be an awareness that there is now a constellation of the archetypal imagery of divination, the element shared by the two brothers. This brings about the possibility of the whole hermetic analytical situation being taken over by Apollo and his oracular, divinatory way of predicting events.

Apollo tells Hermes that the divination of the three virginal sisters can be taught to mortals. Probably he is referring to something that is more commonly taught than we think, and of which we have all learned a bit. But one also suspects that Apollo's divination can be taught too: oracular interpretation of dreams, plans for long-distance actions, moral rectifications, etc.

> To communicate with Mars, converse with spirits,
> To report the behaviour of the sea monster,
> Describe the horoscope, haruspicate or scry,
> Observe disease in signatures, evoke
> Biography from the wrinkles of the palm
> And tragedy from fingers; release omens
> By sortilege, or tea leaves, riddle the inevitable
> With playing cards; fiddle with pentagrams
> Or barbituric acids, or dissect
> The recurrent image into pre-conscious terrors –
> To explore the womb, or tomb, or dreams;
> all these are usual...[37]

All these are usual indeed and, as we have seen, have archetypes to support them. And if they have appeared throughout the history of humankind, then they appear in the analytical consulting room. We have to become aware of the way in which they appear in our psyche and their implications in what follows.

At the conclusion of the Hymn, Hermes receives a last office: "... that he only should be the appointed messenger to Hades...,"[38] an office that gives him the rank of being the only Olympian to deal directly with the depths and mysteries of the realm of the dead; a specific and important task, psychologically speaking. I am sure that by now the reader is sufficiently acquainted with Hermes' personality and qualities to appreciate that he is ideally suited to this ministry,

---

37. T.S. Eliot, *Four Quartets* (Faber and Faber: London, 1944), The Dry Salvages, p. 32.
38. "Homeric Hymn to Hermes," *op. cit.*, p. 405.

especially through his connection to the level of the primitive man in a way no other Olympian can match.

The task of guiding the soul into the underworld cannot be minimized or omitted from psychology and, even less, from psychotherapy. Death is death – the always fearful opposite of life – in spite of the fact that our culture has systematically repressed what death is to the psyche. It is a repression with a tragic background, in that Aeschylus, in the fifth century B.C., had already discerned the Promethean repression of death.

"Yes. I caused men no longer to foresee their death."[39]

It is a formidable line that with hindsight seems prophetic; it also enables us to insight the source of this historical repression and its re-inforcement throughout Christianity. During our own times, the repression has reached such an extreme that the rituals, emotions, and sentiments surrounding death, with all their accompanying imagery, have almost disappeared. With the collapse and failure of traditional religious values concerning death, those ethical and moralistic values weighed on the scales of heaven and hell, a psychic tension of opposites, central to Western man's religious beliefs, was dissipated. But no imagination arose to take its place as regards man's psychic life, emotions, and pathology. Since the end of the Middle Ages, religion has been more concerned with its secular side than with its religious mysteries and death. Death is no longer the concern of communal religion. Modern man is alone in the face of his death – a fact we have to accept. If, however, we look at his desolation in the face of death from a psychology of depth, it has been to man's gain, because it provides him with the freedom to make death his own imaginative and intimate concern, to become better acquainted with his own images and emotions concerning death, thus enriching his psychic life. Now this is obviously

39. Aeschylus, *Prometheus Bound* (Penguin: Harmondsworth, 1961), p. 28

important, my aim being to arrive at death as having a central place in psychotherapy.

And this same freedom allows me to imagine death in that "dark night-time" alluded to in the Hymn; to let my own primitiveness 'read' that dark night-time as it would a piece of mythical thinking: primordial man, full of awe and horror, realizing death as death, the devastating shock that brought the first awareness of himself, the shock that began to make him human – the awakening of the instinct of reflection, the beginning of psychic life, culture, and religious belief. The historians of prehistory, paleontologists, anthropologists, animal behaviorists, and biologists have provided us with enough background to imagine how there was a sudden awareness of death, a shock to man's nature that created a specific human consciousness, – the reflection of death in the other, probably stirred to life by the animal death ritual, a linking of the death ritual with an incipient imagination: the beginning of mythical thinking and poetry. But let us stretch our imagination further and see that primordial man, out of his awareness of death and pressured by his imagination, begins to speak his first articulate words. Death became not simply an animal ritual: the spoken myth was on its way. I wish to see this specific awareness of death as an essential aspect of the complexities contributing to the psycho-biological changes out of which speech was born.[40] I believe this attempt to penetrate the dark night-time is a valid intuition, in view of my interest to expand psychotherapy by putting death in the foreground. At the same time, the dark night-time can be imagined as a realm in our own nature, where the imagination has its

40. Modern man's studies of his beginnings as a human being, the studies on which I base my thought, undoubtedly make for a passionate and fascinating field for reflection. The literature's main interest is centered on hunting as the origin of speech. I simply want to include man's awareness of his death as an important ingredient – the most imaginative, metaphysical if you like, but for me the most psychical – over and above the speculations in this respect.

deepest roots, where the primordial images are stored that mobilize what today we call psyche – our instincts and psychosomatic emotional body; as well as the many other imaginative conceptions of psyche. Man's first awareness of death formed his basic psyche.[41]

Keeping in mind this imaginative approach to death and speech, its psychic consciousness, let us turn to modern psychology. Historically, the scientific mind, under the pressure of mental illness, took over man's need to 'investigate' his psyche. The relation between cause and effect stimulated a new interest in psychic life. At the same time, a vast bulk of knowledge was built up into what we might call a 'psychiatric culture.' Such is the weight and reality of this culture that it has already become a historical complex in today's world, subject to the same geographical, racial, religious, and historical pressures and conflicts. It has undoubtedly become a very important complex. We have only to consider how it has become the most powerful lense through which to see into man's nature and behavior. It has become indispensable. At a more familiar level, the psychiatric cultural complex explains the infinite psychotherapeutic conceptions, not to mention the pharmakos that appears every day in the neuro-chemical laboratories.

As the century draws to its close, this psychiatric complex affects the whole world, but, needless to say, especially those persons who are professionally involved in it. The world is more and more inundated by a profusion of theories and therapeutical techniques, and the complex continues to expand. Just as with any other complex, we can be identified with it, unconscious of it, possessed by it, etc. Moreover, like any other complex, it can be destructive, and only to be dealt with in the way Jung taught us: by circumambulating it or, as Hermes classically does, by keeping one foot in and the other out. It is evident, however, that many students of

41. E.R. Dodds, *The Greeks and the Irrational* (Univ. California Press: Berkeley, 1968), Chap. V, "The Greek Shamans and the Origin of Puritanism."

psychology have been possessed by the profusion of theories and drowned in the complex, or have dealt with it in the most usual way a complex is dealt with: through power. Now power substitutes or replaces what should be our main concern – psyche. The only sound relationship we can have to this complex, the only way to protect our psyche, is to try to keep the right distance from it, to thieve from it hermetically, or to barter with it.

There is another predominant element in the psychiatric culture, stronger and more archetypally defined than the modern scientific mind: the *puer aeternus;* one could even say these two elements have fused. Only Jung and his followers have made the puer aeternus their concern; but they have viewed the puer in terms of a two-headed archetype – the opposition of puer and senex, childhood and adolescence versus adulthood and old age. Now my interest here is to see the puer in opposition to the chthonic Hermes, messenger to the realm of the dead, who would be the link between the puer and the senex while remaining in exclusive opposition to the flying puer.

It is only in terms of this mixture – the bringing together of the scientific mind and the flying puer – that we can have a more psychological view of the complexes ruling the psychiatric culture and the studies of psychology. The cause of mental illness, as the scientifically-minded pioneers tended to see it, was to be found in childhood, the personal childhood of the sufferer, thus giving an imprint to psychology and reinforcing the notion that psychotherapy (the concern of this book) is being limited to the causalism of childhood. A great part of the psychiatric culture, psychoanalysis, and more than a few of Jung's followers have focused their interest primarily on childhood, to avoid saying they are trapped in the complex of the scientific mind and the ruling psychology of the puer aeternus, the two predominant components of the psychiatric culture. This focus on childhood can be seen as a projection of the puer, giving carte blanche to science. To look at this complex more psychologically, it can be viewed as a modern worship of the old religious puer, today's science at the altar of the puer, a perverse worship out of context. I say out of context because we live in a world already unbalanced, archetypally, due to the dominating complexities of the ascending puer. Here this archetype can be viewed as an important aspect of ruling collective consciousness (the entire history of Western man bears witness to it) – a very twisted psychology or sheer madness. Moreover, the dominating force of the puer in the field of psychology does not allow for other psychological conceptions, even in Jungian psychology, in which a great part of Jung's legacy has still to find its proper course. For the puer only learns in relation to what fits into his archetypal configuration, meaning that any knowledge coming from another archetype is automatically translated into his own puer aeternus vision. He can only see in terms of his archetypal puer flying consciousness. It is a consciousness which is able to conceive an abundance of theories and psychologies, but, because of its polarization, it is very far from that medium of consciousness which makes psychotherapy possible, and even farther away from a psychotherapy based on the image of Hermes guiding the soul into the realm of the dead and the many metaphorical possibilities it offers. The psychology of the opposites is alien to the consciousness of the puer aeternus.

There is another ingredient to add to these complexities we are looking at: when modern students of psychology focus their studies on childhood as the cause of mental illness, they place their interest within the limitation of the medical tradition. Now the medical tradition cures in terms of specific illnesses, and is fixed, mythologically, in Asclepius' 'original sin' of rejecting Hades, a rejection that has led to the concretization of rescuing life from death and an artificial prolongation of life as medicine's chief goal. But, at the same time, this attitude has blocked any access on psychotherapy's part to what could bring a more dynamic psychic transformation: death as the primordial psychic mover; even in an illness that can be taken as having been caused, specifically, by the family history (personal com-

plexes). We are beginning to appreciate that there is a
serious archetypal discrepancy between the healing tradition and a psychotherapy concerned with death, with a
chthonic Hermes who can guide the soul into the realm of
the dead.

Let us now turn our attention to how the two most
important men of the psychology of this century
approached death, generally speaking, in relation to
dreams. And here let us remind ourselves that the material
of dreams is the closest expression of what is unknown in
ourselves – the id, the unconscious, the irrational, the
shadow of our nature, etc. Dreams give us information,
either clearly, obscurely, or in riddles, about our psychological state, the direction of our psyche, and even the prognosis of our life. So let us first take a look at how Freud viewed
dreams in which death was present. His view makes for a
primal image in that he was a pioneer and so gave to death
in dreams an indelible imprint, profoundly influencing
what came later. When Freud conceived the death of a
parental figure, or brother, or close friend, as an expression
of a wish fulfillment, we can appreciate the enormous guilt
the dreamer must have felt, not to mention the total paraly-
sis of his psyche and the power this gave to the analyst. Freud
was the product of a guilt-ridden racial and religious tradition; his view of death as a wish fulfillment was the only
possible coherent approach to support the validity of his
theory of the Oedipus complex; his interpretation of death
in dreams fitted into his theories and interest on childhood.
So in that first imprint, guilt made its mark on the history of
modern psychotherapy, and death's metaphorical message
to the psyche was lost.

Jung, on the other hand, based the main conception of
his psychotherapeutical psychology on midlife changes, and
so his approach to death material in dreams was to take it as
an indication of an initiatory movement, as a preparation
for the second half of life, as the beginning of a closer and
more vivid relationship to one's own end. This intuitive
vision of midlife and the emphasis on the preparation for

death is obviously more psychic than the reductive narrowness of the focus on childhood. The end is more important than the beginning. Jung moved dreams with death material into prospective speculations, into eschatalogical conceptions influenced by the history of Western culture in relation to the immortality of the soul and the after-life. Modern scholars have tracked down the roots of such conceptions to primitive man's shamanism, and hypothesized that they were assimilated to Pythagorean and Orphic doctrines, as well as later to the ascensional side of Christianity. It seems that Jung was psychologically in this tradition.

The way in which Freud and Jung dealt mainly with death dreams gives us a view of an essential aspect of their psyches and personalities; likewise, in psychotherapy, a patient's conception of death – how he fantasizes his imagery of death, his emotional attitude towards it – makes a picture that could be viewed as a diagnosis, so to say, of his psyche, and also as a prognosis of his psychic movement. In themselves, death dreams offer a spectrum of possibilities ranging from diagnosis and psychic movement to a psychotherapy of depth or its conclusion.

Archetypally and psychotherapeutically, the appointment of Hermes as the guide of the soul into the underworld has a very different connotation to the general conceptions of Freud and Jung. 'Archetypal' means that it belongs to human nature: we all have a Hermes to guide the soul into the realm of the dead, and the conception of this office varies with each person's psychic entity, religious background, culture, and complexes, or with the different fantasies, images, emotions, and sentiments concerning death. But more than this, death could be understood as a constancy in the psyche, and dreams of death as touching our animal/instinctive/primitive, mythical complexes, since my interest is to attach these dreams to the oldest of our complexes – that dark night-time. Psychotherapeutically, this means that death imagery can appear in the therapeutic here and now, can erupt into the therapeutical process at any given time, even in the first session, regardless of the patient's age, whether in a pathological depression or not, burdened by a recent death, or haunted by a past death which has left its mark on the soul's memory. The appearance of death in psychotherapy is a happening, with its own urgency and emotions and, because of its depth, it offers an imaginative perspective of the patient without parallel. However, it can throw off balance the most skilled and experienced analyst. In general, there is a given and stereotyped attitude to death, the analyst remaining rigidly within his own cultural conceptions and so failing to respond with an imagination that could match up to the imagery of death constellated in the patient. Moreover, the uncanniness of the appearance of images of death can move the analyst into the concretization of a possible actual death, an attitude stemming from the emotions carried by the word, 'death' and from aspects of the healer archetype concerning death which we have already referred to.

Hermes as messenger to the realm of the dead allows us also to approach depression as a constant level in our nature. We know the psychic imagery of death and depression are so akin they often overlap. If, archetypally, the flying puer aeternus is in opposition to insighting death, then obviously he is in opposition to depression. When a puer-dominated consciousness needs to confront death in a religious sense, there is the immediate tendency to jump out of the emotional reality of death. The religious history of Western man has been more concerned with resurrection than with death. In a similar way and in a more everyday therapeutic context, when the depressive side of our nature demands to be present in life, the flying puer tends to reject its presence – to resist staying in the depression or to anticipate immediately the post-depressive stage; a typical example of how the puer moves any insight or experience into his own archetypal design, revealing the inflated pretentiousness and, at the same time, the sad limitation of his vision.

Western man is biased towards activity and effort, a bias that blinds him to any insights into death and depression as archetypal, as part of his nature. Modern medicine sees the time when healing was conceived in terms of rest and repose at spas, beaches, and mountains, in terms of a pause indirectly providing access to depression, as a very remote and decrepit past. We live in times when healing is conceived in terms of weekend operations, with assurances that the patient can be back at his activities by Monday morning; in terms of weekends of marathonic psychotherapy, with assurances of a quick elimination of hang-ups. On top of man's mounting activities, the healing trend is towards exercise, jogging, and so forth, a trend that has become a slogan and fits into easy onesided expectations: the promise of better health, a stronger heart, and a longer happier life. In other words, there is a total rejection of the association of illness and depression, and of the necessity of providing hermetic indirection into depression. This is commonplace in our modern technological society, a sort of healing that does not allow even the minimum time for the psyche to become aware of what is happening to its own nature and body. To rest, repose, and to depress have become the most difficult of achievements. In reality, we need the mood of "Sunday, Bloody Sunday," to provide a drop of the depression and its imagery that is so lacking. Without depression, we cannot exist; it is a basic component of life; it is archetypal. Depression has become desperate, so to speak, seeking an outlet that is easily discerned in psychological tensions and conflicts, and in psychosomatic conditions. Only a minority of healers are concerned with this situation: the odd psychotherapist who, in his standard work, includes the slow incubatory movement of the psyche, the process of slowing down; depression is central to any healing process.

Nevertheless, depression is also an illness, according to its quantity and complexity in a person. It can be a psychic depression, a sign of serious psychosomatic illness, or a sign of imminent death. And, in considering a depressive condition, the many devices and remedies created by the 'psychiatric culture' mentioned before – from electric shock to the latest anti-depressive pill – cannot be ignored.

With respect to depression, my interest is to address the practitioner, not the patient, because it is obvious that a psychotherapeutic view of it depends on the analyst's consciousness of depression, including his own. To apprehend what the last image of the Hymn intimates for a therapy of depression and to let Hermes' imagination deal with it, within the archetypal limits of the image, it is essential to have an anthropological and religious culture. And although, as was just mentioned, psychopathology's bulk of knowledge cannot be disregarded, the therapist should appreciate that depression is a natural expression of certain complexities in accordance with each person's nature and psychic entity. But, again, we have to realize just how difficult it is for us to accept our nature. Depression was important to Jung's healing process, and those of us who have profited from his teaching know that psychological movement and a state of depression are connected. It is as if it were a pause on nature's part that makes it possible for consciousness to grasp new unconscious contents.

Now let us concentrate imaginatively on the realm to which Hermes is the guide, for not only does it provide us with metaphors, but it can also lead us towards a compensatory psychotherapy. The most immediate compensation to our onesidedness is to be found in the double metaphorical image of depression and death. There can be no psychic transformation without compensatory opposites. Now, in psychotherapy today, we are repeatedly confronted with people who live as if they had no body; as if their body was a totally alien entity. We know that historical and religious repression, philosophical and scientific conceptions, as well as, last but not least, modern technology, have alienated us from what should be psychic – our body. It is evidently not easy to acknowledge that our illnesses reside in our bodies, just as psyche resides in our bodies. It seems the aim of psychotherapy, in this respect, is to propitiate the feeling of living in one's own body, seemingly such an easy achievement, especially today when the body has become so fashionable. But, if we consider how history has rejected the psychic emotional body, as with depression, it is very difficult indeed.

From the classical literature and scholarship concerning Dionysus,[42] we gather that he is the god who stands for the psychical and emotional body, as well as the feelings of one's own body. Both mythologically and historically, Dionysus is the most rejected of all the gods; and we know how systematically Western man has rejected his emotional body, because of the ascensional spiritual complexes of Christianity. So we can take Dionysus' imagination as a metaphor for that repressed psychical and emotional body about which we know so little, and which pertains to the imagery surrounding Hermes' appointment as messenger to the realm of the dead – the dead body, the nonexistent body of today's man. Whatever speculations we may have as regards Dionysus and Hades being the same, the association is implicit in the relationship we have been making between death, depression, and the psychic body (a body psyche can feel). Here is where Hermes comes in, guiding the soul into the underworld, an image which implies a gravitational movement. There is, of course, no guarantee of achieving this compensatory movement towards a psychic body, into procuring a ground where our psychosomatic suffering would not be so terribly alien; it has to be seen as a hermetic happening.

A psychotherapy interested in moving psyche into the body requires, as we have been working out, a hermetic consciousness, a familiarity with hermetic timing and indirection, a reasonable easiness with depression, no preconceived ideas, but a reliance on words and imagination with regard to death as the prime psychic mover. If death is at the origin of religious and mythical thinking and poetry, then

42. For those not versed in the literature concerning Dionysos and for an insight into the psychical and emotional body, I recommend Ivan M. Linforth, *The Arts of Orpheus* (Univ. of California Press: Berkeley, 1941), especially Chapter V, "Myth of the Dismemberment of Dionysus"; and W.B. Stanford, *Greek Tragedy and the Emotions* (Routledge & Kegan Paul: London, 1983).

when death is put into words, therapy through speech, the 'talking cure,' has its deepest significance where gestures and words can be understood as therapeutic in themselves, unpressured by the weight of history, and where there is the possible happening of a therapeutic dialogue that touches fundamental complexes – death and speech.

The term *psuchogogia* means, literally, a psyche led by itself and in this there is a specific emotion. The last image of the Homeric "Hymn to Hermes" fits very well with the principle of *psuchogogia:* Hermes leading the psyche, without any intervention, into its own essence.

Chapter III

A Tale of Homer and Picasso

There is another tale in which Hermes, though he is not the main character, plays an important role. This story gives us images for moving our study further, and it keeps a certain sequence within our line of thought. It is the gracious tale told by Homer in the *Odyssey* of the adultery of Aphrodite, who was married at the time to Hephaestus.

Aphrodite and Ares were having a secret love-affair. It happened that the Sun saw "their loving embraces" and went immediately to inform Hephaestus:

> ... who, when he heard the galling truth, went straight to his workshop with his heart full of evil thoughts, laid his great anvil on the smithy and forged a chain network that could neither be broken nor undone, so as to keep them prisoners forever. His fury with Ares inspired him as he worked, and when the snare was finished he went to the room where his bed was laid and threw the netting right around the bedposts. A number of further lengths were attached to the rafters over-head and hung down light as gossamer and quite invisible even to the blessed gods. It was a masterful piece of cunning work.[1]

Hephaestus then pretended to leave for Lemnos. Meanwhile Ares watched him go and, at once, went to Aphrodite, who was delighted to see him, desiring "... nothing better than to sleep with him; so the two went to the bed and lay

---

1. Homer, *The Odyssey*, trans. Rieu, *op. cit.*, p. 129.

down. Whereupon the netting ... fell around them in such a way that they could not move or lift a limb. They found too late that there was no escape."[2] The Sun, acting as Hephaestus' spy, informed him of the situation and the lame god hurried back in anguish, confronted the two lovers, shouting so loudly in his terrible rage that all the gods could hear him. His pent-up resentment exploded and he threatened to keep Aphrodite and Ares imprisoned on the bed until Zeus returned the gifts Hephaestus had given him in order to win Aphrodite for his wife.

> His shouts brought the gods trooping to the house with the bronze door. Up came Poseidon the Earthshaker; Hermes, the bringer of luck; and the archer king, Apollo; but the goddesses, constrained by feminine modesty, all stayed at home. There they stood then, in front of the doors ... and when they caught sight of Hephaestus' clever device a fit of uncontrollable laughter seized these happy gods.[3]

They made joking comments and then:

> ... King Apollo, Son of Zeus, turned to Hermes and said: 'Hermes, you that are Son of Zeus, Ambassador and Giver of good things, would you care, though held in those unyielding shackles, to lie in bed by golden Aphrodite's side?'
> To which the Giant-slayer replied: 'Apollo, my royal Archer, there is nothing I should relish more. Though the chains that kept me prisoner were three times as many, though all you gods and all the goddesses were looking on, yet would I gladly sleep by golden Aphrodite's side.'
> His jest raised another laugh from all the gods except Poseidon, who was not amused, but kept urging the great smith Hephaestus to free Ares from the net.
> 'Let him go,' he insisted: 'and I promise you that he himself shall make full and proper atonement as required by you, in the presence of the immortal gods.'[4]

2. *Ibid.*, p. 130.
3. *Ibid.*, pp. 130-131.
4. *Ibid.*, p. 131.

Hephaestus protested that Ares might "shuffle out of his debt." So Poseidon said that if Ares absconded, he would pay the debt himself. The lame god felt that he could not refuse such an offer and freed the lovers.

This delightful story gives us an impression of how Hermes graciously and in the most overt way, to the point of shamelessness, fantasizes about sexuality, showing us a sexuality easily carried. Moreover, Hermes is not at all bothered by revealing his fantasies in front of the rest of the gods. The image shows clearly that Hermes can accept the pornographic play of the psyche. This image portrays the two extreme reactions to the same image – Hermes, who accepts the fantasy totally, and Poseidon, who is revolted by it. The image shows a libidinous attitude on Hermes' part and a strongly repressive one on that of Poseidon. These are the two attitudes which I would like to discuss.

First let us take a closer look at Poseidon's attitude. He seems to react in a prudish and scandalized way, unable to enjoy the sexual humor in the situation as the other gods do. Is his attitude betraying sexual inhibition? Is he the one who represses sexuality and tries to hide it, the one who shows a scandalized and puritanical attitude in front of what could be called a pornographic image?

It is also not difficult to see characteristic elements of compulsion in the god. Poseidon rules the sea and rivers and springs, which are never at rest even when seemingly calm, so he is a propitious image for insighting the natural function of compulsion. We may remember that he built the walls of Troy "with such labour,"[5] which is an image of both compulsion and protection. The Poseidon element in the sexual story recounted by Homer shows repulsion towards the imagery of sexuality and a compulsion to be rid of it as quickly as possible.

We can further our insights into Poseidon's psychology from the way in which he wants to resolve the situation in the story. He even goes as far as to offer to pay Hephaestus

5. Homer, *The Iliad*, trans. Rieu, *op. cit.*, p. 143.

what he demands for freeing Ares, though, in reality, this is not his business as it was to Zeus that Hephaestus made his demand. We have seen this sort of reaction many times, a puritanical and prudish attitude which tries at any cost to cover up what, for this archetype, is a scandal. So, on the one hand, we have a psychology which views this kind of image as scandalous and tries to dispose of it immediately, and, on the other, the psychology of blackmail, in which there is the willingness to pay in order to cover up the scandal. The classic tale offers both.

We are looking into the archetypal background of trying to cover up and pay when a sexual situation (image) is seen from a predominantly prudish side of the psyche. In psychotherapy it happens frequently that a sexual episode in the patient's life is seen from Poseidon's prudish point of view. The patient tries to pay an endless psychological blackmail for it and the psychotherapist, though falling into the same archetypal pattern, being caught, unconsciously feeds this blackmail.

Let us also consider that the fathers of modern psychology were scientifically-minded, prudish Jewish men who lived the Diaspora during the last episode of the Austro-Hungarian Empire, a time imbued with Victorian puritanism.[6] Inevitably they viewed sexual imagery from the angle which was historically predominant in them. No one can avoid his own history and so, naturally, they brought it into psychoanalysis. Their reaction to sexuality was close to that of Poseidon in the tale; they saw it as sick, in keeping with the vision of their time (sexual trauma) and they also sought to release it from its chains. They tried to 'cure' that sickness and 'control' the psyche which presented it to them.

Now, let us return to the tale and look at it from the point of view of Hermes who, in the same situation, shows a very

6. In the history of Western culture, the Victorian age was only one period of the conflict between chastity (Artemis) and sexual desire (Aphrodite). It is an archetypal conflict which existed long before Christianity, as we can see in Euripides' *Hippolytus*.

different attitude to that of Poseidon. The way he fantasizes about going to bed with Aphrodite and the amused participation of the other gods, except for Poseidon, tells us a lot about the fantasy-erotica that this god constellates. We are told that the goddesses were not there, though Hermes says that he would not be ashamed of going to bed with Aphrodite in front of them too. He is probably hinting that with the gracious shamelessness of his sexual fantasies, he is able to convey sexual images to those lady divinities also.

If we read again the image in the tale, we can see that there is a sexual situation in which the three main characters, Aphrodite, Ares, and Hephaestus, are caught. Just as Ares and Aphrodite are literally chained, so too is Hephaestus in that he conceived the net. We can detect that the other characters in the story were caught also by the situation. Apollo, assuming his distant, rather lofty attitude, enquires of Hermes, like a modern researcher on sexuality might do, whether he would like to be in the same situation as Ares, and he believes that with his detached questioning he is not caught. But it seems to me that his question in itself implies that he is caught. In any case, the different reactions of these gods to the situation gives us a spectrum of how each one in his own way is caught by the same sexual image.

The only god who is not caught is, obviously, Hermes, because he gladly starts to fantasize the situation, and takes it even further by saying that even with three times the number of chains he would happily go to bed with Aphrodite. Furthermore, he would do it in front of all the other gods and goddesses. Here we have another beautiful example of how Hermes is never caught. He accepts the situation he has in front of him, but he is able to fantasize about it and take it to an even further extreme, a way of fantasizing worth noting for psychology. In psychotherapy, when it becomes obvious that the patient is totally fixated on a sexual episode, hysterically blaming psychic stagnation and mediocrity on a sexual episode, one response the analyst could make would be to follow Hermes' model: to accept the situation into which the patient is trying to trap his psyche (and the analytical process) and in fantasizing about it take it even further, thus depotentiating the patient's fixation and avoiding being caught in the blackmail. This sort of response could possibly procure some psychic movement.

This image in Homer's tale offers many possibilities for psychological reflection. One component in the image is adultery, and adultery invariably brings about jealousy. There is no doubt that Hephaestus is jealous. In the previous chapter we discussed a mythological scene in which jealousy was mentioned, but it was jealousy with the connotation of envy; here, in this story, there is sexual jealousy, treated by Homer as a delightful game of the gods, told with the humor found in a comedy to give a certain distance to jealousy and so deflating the seriousness of its emotional impact on the soul. Jealousy is an emotional component in human nature, and when it arises and possesses the personality, it can be very destructive. Homer shows that all the gods feel jealousy and sometimes, following the interchangeability of the two words jealousy and envy, one feels a mixture of the two. The fact that the gods can be jealous attests to how deeply ingrained the emotion must be in human nature. Hephaestus, knowing his wife is committing adultery, is sexually jealous, but we can speculate that, in being a lame god, he is also envious of Ares' virility, a god, we could say, who, among other things, has the attribute of male aggressiveness. By taking into consideration the mixture of jealousy and envy, the tale becomes more complex and more profitable to study for psychotherapy, where we are used to dealing with jealousy – ranging from its very destructive side (suicide or homicide) to the other extreme, where it is an awakening of dormant emotions.

Western culture has Shakespeare's masterpiece *Othello,* a deep and complex presentation of jealousy and envy in human nature, resulting in tragic destruction; but there is another work, not such a masterpiece as Shakespeare's, one of Cervantes' minor works in *Novelas Ejemplares* "La Gitanilla" in which la Gitanilla was wise because she knew about jealousy. (I am always amazed by the way in which these two geniuses dealt with jealousy.) These two works reveal the wide range of the emotion of jealousy in the human soul: from destruction to wisdom. Between these two extremes are all the varied manifestations of this emotion, experienced uniquely in each soul. Probably in the times of Shakespeare and Cervantes, Western man was more able to accept his jealousy than we are today; he knew more about it. In today's psychotherapy, this very important psychic component is presented under modern man's pretension of having his emotional life under 'control,' that these sort of silly feelings have been left behind, that there are more important things in life than to be jealous of a wife or lover; or jealousy is not even noticed and there is a complete inability to live jealousy in a relationship, allowing us to diagnose a lack of emotional body, which in itself reveals the condition of the whole personality. This pretentious denial of jealousy can be added to the repressive onesidedness of modern man. So jealousy, such a fundamental emotion in human relations, takes its revenge from below and, from one day to the next, destroys the relationship under the unconscious guise of the most handy pretext. At other times, the revenge comes in the nature of depressions and psychosomatizations. By tactfully welcoming jealousy into psychotherapy, we are moving the psychotherapeutic situation into an acceptance of one of the most repressed emotions. It has happened more than once that through jealousy the patient begins to understand his inner emotions, opening the way to compensation.

These two passions, envy and jealousy, deserve a more thorough treatment than I am able to give them here.[7] Modern psychotherapy's general view of jealousy has been dominated by reduction, reducing it to the parental triangle, showing power in the reductive method which pretends

7. I have not discussed the irrationality of jealousy in the text because the image does not lend itself to this; but jealousy is one of the most common ways in which the irrational appears in psychotherapy, bringing the first acceptance and insights into the irrational part of the psyche.

to 'know' about the cause of emotion, dissecting the soul or drying out the well of emotion. In reality, jealousy and envy call for, if not the treatment of our two geniuses, then at least the respect they demand for being of such profound importance in human nature.

But let us come back to Homer's tale which is centered in a trio situation. It shows, apparently, a very male hetero-sexual attitude on the part of both Hephaestus and Ares and a typically female coquetry on the part of Aphrodite. How-ever, the psychological reality is a trio situation. Although, as I said before, the psychology of the trio has mostly been seen reductively, our aim is to take a good look at it and to train our minds to be ready for its possible constellation in psychotherapy. This approach cannot be taught or learned in terms of training; only life itself, with the help of Hermes, might provide the possibilities for perceiving and insighting the formation of trio images in psychotherapy. We psychol-ogists have to take into account that the analytical psycho-therapeutical eros involves, more often than we think (prob-ably always), a third person, and this third one makes us doubtful about that *temenos* of only analyst and patient. In reality, either hidden or apparent, there is invariably a third, and this third can make different combinations of the trio in the psychotherapeutical transference. When discussing with the patient that third person who is not present, the psychotherapist has to be exceedingly tactful, for this is where his art is at stake, because he does not know whether jealousy and envy are hidden in the constellation, and any indiscriminate reaction from the analyst could disturb the patient's psychic movement. Perhaps what we are discussing has more to do with the art and personal style of the therapist than to the *métier* he is expected to know.

From our reading of Homer's image, it seems that Her-mes is the only one who can move into a delicate situation involving a threesome and its jealousy. As we mentioned before, the other gods were caught by the situation; it appeared to them more as a concretized reality. For the other gods to fantasize a delicate situation such as Hermes can is beyond their archetypal range. They do not have that quality of Hermes which enables him to enter a sexual fantasy (including its sexual reality, if you will) and know how to emerge again. (Hermes gave Ulysses the moly, which enabled him to approach Circe and not get caught in her machinations.) Hermes' ease and lack of embarrassment, when he accepts the idea of going to bed with Aphrodite in front of all the other gods and goddesses, reveals a nature basically able to deal with jealousy. He is able to enter the fantasy of the situation psychologically, accept being one of the components in the threesome and, in spite of this, can re-emerge from the situation.

*
* *

Hermes' fantasy of going to bed in front of all the gods and goddesses gives us an approach from which to consider another psychological issue. Today, pornography has moved so openly into the foreground, and with such a quantitative aspect, that we have a historical perspective from which to bring it into discussion. The collective psyche is desperately trying to say something through this widespread predominance of pornography. Recently an American newspaper reported on a pornographic situation before a judge. His response was to say that he was there to deal with murder, theft, and crime in general but not with this kind of thing. This statement reveals how the law today does not deal with something that only yesterday it condemned. It is the very law which condemned adultery during the time when the pioneers of modern psychology were engaged in their major works.

The vast amount of pornography we see everywhere in our culture makes us realize, and maybe accept, that this vast amount of pornography in the streets is also within us, in our psyche. Maybe what we see outside is merely a tiny, timid expression of the pornographic images within. It is probably this inner pornographic imagery which has induced some therapists to practice psychotherapy through pornography; the fashionable sex therapist practices a psychotherapy through pornography, under the guise of a clean, scientific, sexual teaching. We want to suggest that these pornographic images are archetypal and that in our reaction to their outer appearance, so tremendously concrete, we can detect how big a role they play in our psyche, from the scandalized rejection of Poseidon, and the researcher attitude of Apollo, to the imaginative acceptance of Hermes.

I had a young, very ill, handicapped patient who discovered pornography. From the researcher point of view I observed that out of this discovery there was some development in him. My fantasy/observation about this development was that, in all probability, he was connecting to, and dealing with, one of the greatest psychological discoveries of the century, the discovery which shocked and scandalized Western culture at the time of the Belle Époque, and which is still having repercussions today – Freud's concept of the child as polymorphous and sexually perverse. At the same time, I detected in myself a rather hermetic attitude which accepted the patient's discovery and even went further in my fantasies about it. I accepted his interest in the many forms of sexuality (polymorphous), which evidently brought with it a measure of psychological development, or even healing (the patient was very ill). Frances Yates mentions Peter of Ravenna, "who in his book on artificial memory has suggested the use of libidinous images to the young."[8] It seems to me that my psychotherapeutical attitude was backed up by both Apollo's observation and Hermes' acceptance and extension of the fantasy.

Hermes' fantasy of being seen in bed with Aphrodite by all the other gods, thus allowing the other gods to project their sexuality onto the scene, might induce us to think about polytheism. Our approach to the archetypes views polymorphous sexuality in terms of each god and goddess having his or her own sexuality, and that sexuality varies

8. Yates, *The Art of Memory, op. cit.,* p. 274.

accordingly. (Even Poseidon shows a form of sexuality in being scandalized.) Hermes' fantasy of performing sexually in front of them all is obviously pornographic and, because he accepts being seen, also polymorphous. (He is the lord of the roads, leading to all possible roads.) In his acceptance of being seen by the rest of the gods, he catches their fantasies through their projection of their own sexualities onto him.

Through Homer's image we have been tracking down the idea that sexuality includes the participation of all the gods (all the archetypes). Otherwise we have to accept a monotheistic sexuality backed by the conception of the one God. A monotheistic sexuality could be conceived as being an idealized, conceptualized, even messianic sexuality (all that missionarism around the orgasm, the proper orgasm, the proper sexuality in marriage, etc., and projecting onto this a healing function). Monotheistic sexuality is also a sexuality without images. If sexuality is monotheistic, implicit in this is the exclusion of the many forms which have been so conflictive in a Western culture, built on the basis of a monotheistic religious fantasy which had, nevertheless, a pagan polytheism in its syncretism.

In the journal, *Spring 1971,*[9] a discussion was opened on the subject of monotheism and polytheism. My impression is that this discussion was shortsighted in that none of the contributions, including my own, pointed to the fact that the ultimate conflict between monotheism and polytheism has a sexual root. D.P. Walker in his book, *The Ancient Theology,* reveals how early Christianity had to missionarize a sexuality of its own, a monotheistic sexuality which excluded polytheism by excluding the many sexual forms of the pagan gods.[10]

---

9. *Spring 1971,* (Spring Publications: Zurich and New York, 1971), James Hillman, "Psychology: Monotheistic or Polytheistic," p. 193 and "Responses and Contributions," p. 209.

10. D.P. Walker, *The Ancient Theology* (Cornell Univ. Press: Ithaca, 1972), p. 8.

In this discussion of polymorphism in sexuality I would not like there to be any thought of my promoting or missionarizing a polytheistic sexuality; that would be to see my ideas from a monotheistic point of view. My intention is to bring into discussion the sexual root of the conflict and to see it as a touchstone in psychology and valid for psychotherapy. To see the conflict between polytheism and monotheism and to discuss it on a religious, cultural, and historical level tends to omit this basic root of the conflict. One aspect in the history of Western culture is monotheism's intervention in sexual life. Here we are perhaps touching upon where religion and sex present a similar conflict in psychotherapy.

We need to bear in mind that this conflict between a monotheistic sexuality and polymorphism (all the pagan gods with their different forms of sexuality) appeared from the beginning in this century's psychology and was the inheritance of the same religious/sexual conflict in Western culture. The polymorphously perverse – the sexuality of the many gods of the pagan pantheon – broke through into the puritanical monotheistic Jewish mind, and was conceptualized as the polymorphously perverse child.

We are the inheritors of such concepts, yet we are living in a time when images can tell us more than concepts. Thus the concept of 'polymorphous perverse' seems remote to us today in comparison with the possibilities that images of the polymorphism of the pagan gods can offer psychotherapy. In the narrative, Homer gives a picture of how the different pagan gods connect to a sexual image, and from this we can appreciate that there are many archetypal ways of seeing one sexual image. He enables us to view polymorphism in sexuality, something that the monotheism of our lives has repressed throughout two millennia. There seems to be a confusion between polymorphous sexuality and the achievement of so-called mature sexuality. The latter is seen less in terms of sexuality than in terms of relationship, a notion which stems from a monotheistic attitude. We can conceive of a relationship maturing with time and age, like wine – this maturity containing ups and downs, some shadow and destruction; but to confuse relationship and sexuality is a transposition, a way of looking at sexuality only from the viewpoint of relationship. Sexuality is more than this; it is an instinct with archetypes and complexes behind it, and it is polymorphous since there are different gods, with their various forms of sexuality, in all of us. These forms seek expression at different times during a lifetime, forms to be lived psychically, without our sexuality being fixed to a preconceived model.

Homer's image has provided us with two important elements: *jealousy,* a sometimes irrational emotion of the human soul, covering a spectrum from sheer destruction to the possibility of psychological insight and psychic movement; and pornography, which is an expression of polymorphism and without which, either in fantasy or reality, through expression or rejection, sexualities do not exist. It is difficult to conceive of a solely monotheistic sexuality.

As I said before, a sexuality without polymorphism does not exist. Monotheism needs polymorphous images from which to image its own sexuality and onto which it can project what it imagines it is not. To think in terms of 'normal' sexuality has nothing to do with the archetypes of sexuality or, at least, the images seem to confirm this. We are disposed to read the two elements of jealousy and pornography in the image because the first, jealousy, is so basic an emotion of the soul, and Hephaestus is plainly jealous (though we have merely touched on it within the limitation of the image), and because the second, pornography, Hermes' fantasy, enables us to reflect on its extensive appearance in this part of the century.

Now if we re-read the image we can see that Hephaestus, the technician, forged his device in order to catch and trap something which in reality, he already knew about. He was well aware that his wife was having a love-affair, but that triggered his jealousy. Thus spurred on by his jealousy, he created a device "invisible even to the blessed gods," to catch and reveal what he already knew. In this way he concretized and fixated the image of his jealousy and turned it into a pornographic image. We have a pornographic image of our jealousy, a connection that Homer, whose genius gave us this image, saw from the beginning. As always, the image teaches more psychology than the concept.

*
* *

If Homer's classic image is not enough, let me introduce the Spanish painter, Pablo Picasso (1881-1973). In 1968 he produced a series of engravings that, among his many exuberant creations, are a unique testimony to the sexual fantasy of an old man.[11] People seem to have difficulty in accepting the fact that an old man has sexual fantasies, just as there has been difficulty in accepting the sexuality of children, a difficulty that has brought enormous confusion to the studies of psychology. It is as if there is something in Western man which distorts sexuality, that is unable to accept it as an inherent part of human nature which accompanies us throughout a lifetime. This becomes obvious in comparative studies of other cultures. In our Western culture, Christianity has dealt with sexuality in a very twisted way, and therefore the approach to an old man's sexuality is in derogatory terms such as 'dirty old man,' a reference only to the external expression of that sexuality, with no consideration of the psychic activity in the sexual instinct.

Picasso's late series of engravings reflect the erotic fantasies of his old age, and the impact of his art forces us to think about sexual fantasy at this time of life. He broadens our vision and verifies once more our insights into the validity of exploring the psychic complexities of old age. T.S. Eliot said, "Old men ought to be explorers."[12] So as explorers let us approach the sexual imagery of Picasso as he imagined it

---

11. 347 Gravures: 16.3.68 – 5.10.68, Galerie Louise Leiris, 18 décembre 1968 – 1er février 1969. (Catalogue No. 23, Série A, Maîtres Imprimeurs Draeger Frères, 1968).

12. Eliot, *Four Quartets, op. cit.,* "East Coker," V, p. 22.

when he was close to ninety years old. For it tells us the story of an old age lived in a way quite different than is usually imagined.

In the series of engravings that I am going to discuss, we are struck by how Picasso reflected his old age through the erotic senility in the image of a pope, thus forcing us to reassess the creative dynamism of a genius at the sunset of his life. Besides being a great contribution to the studies of man's culture, these engravings can teach us psychology. Their imagery could be called archetypal, especially if we connect it to the Homeric roots of our culture, though, inevitably, it is archetypal within the limitations of Picasso's own psyche and history. In the superabundance of his creation, he expresses both the limitations and potential of his creative imagination; its variety never ceases to surprise us, and the historicity of many of his images is striking. He was a Spanish, Mediterranean man, a man very much in touch with that hermetic primitiveness that is such an important aspect of this study of Hermes. This series of engravings gives us a vivid impression of how, through Renaissance legends and imagery, his genius captured the basic conflicts of the Renaissance man's soul; and how, through living his own sexuality psychically, he connected to the archetypal contents we are dealing with in this chapter, namely, sexual fantasies, pornography, and threesome psychology. The sexuality of his imagery suggests that sexual images are central to an old man's exploration, just as they are present in any exploration.

In the 1968 catalogue of engravings, Picasso displays a variety of images, most of them with a strong sexual content, whose dominating theme is that of La Celestina (the procuress of sexual fantasies), based on *La Celestina,* the tragicomedy of Fernando de Rojas, 1492. But being Picasso, he touches on many other themes familiar to him: the theatre (*Commedia dell'Arte*); the circus, with its fools and freaks; the bullfight; and Spanish folkloric scenes with guitarists and women with panderetas. However, the engravings (296-315) that are relevant for linking Picasso with our tale of Homer,

were added to the end of the catalogue of the Galerie
Louise Leiris as they were not shown in the exhibition, no
doubt due to prudishness. We are going to take four engravings from this series, as they are sufficient for tracing a
movement, a kind of dive of the creative psyche into the
memory stored in the unconscious. These engravings do
not differ much from a series of dreams in which the
dreaming psyche descends (so to say) and connects to
unconscious contents which are constellated at a given time.
If, in the Homeric tale, we have a group of gods looking at a
god and goddess trapped together in bed, here, many
centuries later, we see a Renaissance pope, the highest
religious dignitary of Christendom, watching a painter and
his model in erotic phallic situations; and Picasso conveys
the psychological drama that is taking place inside the pope.
The Homeric tale tells us a bit about how pagan man dealt
with sexuality religiously; and Picasso tells us about the
inner drama that sexuality provokes in the Western religious
man.

In engraving 297, the attitude of the pope-voyeur [Plate
5] clearly shows a certain innocence. In the next engraving
(298) [Plate 6], however, the impact of the image in front of
him is such that his face has become totally mad. Picasso
shows us what happened to a traditional, religious, virginal
man during the Renaissance, when sexuality, systematically
repressed since the beginning of Christianity, appeared at
the window of history. It made its appearance as a fantasy
guiding a cavalcade of pagan images, which likewise had
been severely repressed but were there in man's nature
waiting to reappear. Viewing the sequence is akin to the
experience of psychotherapy. Deep transformation requires
the impact of images that shock the *status quo* of consciousness; it also requires a psyche that can withstand such
images. In engraving 300, the pope-voyeur has a third eye in
his forehead [Plate 7], and we realize the scene cannot
simply be reduced to erotic imagery. There is something to
be learned: the pope has learned from all the drama and
madness to which his curiosity has subjected him. We, too,

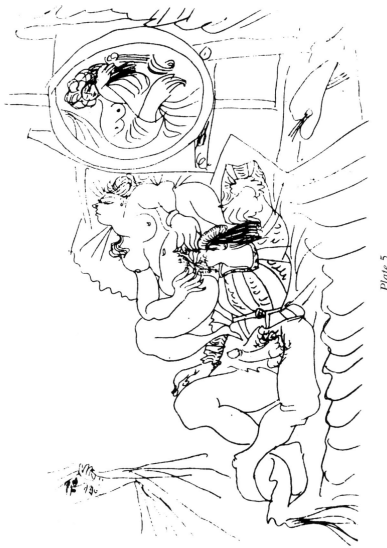

Plate 5

Plate 6

Plate 7

Plate 8

can learn from Picasso's imagery. In engraving 306, the pope has become calm and his dignity is restored [Plate 8]: Picasso depicts him as a patron of the arts, choosing the paintings that, later, were to become the heritage of Western man's art and history.

As we follow the sequence in our four engravings, we become aware that the members of the trio – the pope, the painter, and the model – are not figments of Picasso's imagination, but are modelled on a Renaissance legend: Raphael Sanzio, another painter of genius; la Fornarina, a beautiful model; and the Pope.

In Homer's passage, as I attempted to discuss, there is an image of Aphrodite and Ares chained in bed by Hephaestus' device, and the rest of the gods are looking at the scene and reacting to it within the archetypal reactions of their godhead. Among Picasso's engravings is another trio out of which he creates a religious, mythological, and historical résumé. What was religion in Homer, expressed by way of a joyful mythological narrative, in Picasso is historical. Both Homer and Picasso suggest different ways of looking at life, art, beauty, and psychology through a threesome psychology with its manifold possibilities of jealousy, pornography, and the 'perverted' polymorphism of these two geniuses in old age.

I would like my reflections on this theme to be taken as an invitation to approach sexuality within its archetypal, religious, and historical background, and to accept art, so neglected and misunderstood by psychology – from Homer to Picasso – as the instrumentation that can add some 'gusto' to the appearance of sexuality (pornography, if you want) in psychotherapy. As we know, there was a time in history – the Renaissance – when Western man lived all the imagery of this conflict, and it could be lived again (perhaps we are living it), at least within the limits of the analytical consulting rooms of modern psychotherapy.

Chapter IV

A Tale of Dryops and the Birth of Pan

In the Homeric "Hymn to Pan," we find a passage concerning Hermes in which this god is in the particular situation of being in servitude to a mortal.

The *Homeric Hymn to Pan* tells of Hermes coming to Arcadia:

> They sing of the blessed gods and high Olympus and choose to tell of such a one as luck-bringing Hermes above the rest, and how he is the swift messenger of all the gods, and how he came to Arcadia, the land of many springs and mother of flocks, there where his sacred place is as god of Cyllene. For there, though a god, he used to tend curly-fleeced sheep in the service of a mortal man, because there fell on him and waxed strong melting desire to wed the rich-tressed daughter of Dryops, and there he brought about the merry marriage. And in the house she bore Hermes a dear son who from his birth was marvellous to look upon, with goat's feet and two horns – a noisy, merry-laughing child.[1]

This child was Pan.

Callimachus recorded the similar situation of Hermes' brother Apollo, in servitude to a mortal king.

> Phoebus and Nomius we call him, ever since the time when by Amphrysus he tended the yoke-mares, fired with love of young Admetus.[2]

---

1. *Hesiod, The Homeric Hymns and Homerica, op. cit.*, XIX, "To Pan," p. 445.
2. *Callimachus, Hymns and Epigrams*, Loeb Classical Library, trans. A.W. Mair (London: Heinemann, 1912), Hymn II, "To Apollo," p. 53.

Now the difference between these two styles of male servitude has been observed by Kerényi, who says of Hermes:

> A story resembling that of Apollo's servitude to King Admetos in Thessaly was told also of Hermes... The story concerning Hermes, on the other hand, was set in Arcadia. Hermes pastured sheep for a mortal master, and whilst so doing, fell in love with a nymph, the "nymph of Dryops." It is not stated that Dryops was Hermes' mortal master, but he seems to have been so.[3]

Of Apollo, Kerényi says:

> In a later version of the story of Apollo's servitude to Admetos, the two were bound together by love. There were many love-stories concerning Apollo, the greater number and the most famous of which ended tragically – whether the object of the god's love was a boy or a girl. The reason that boys were numbered amongst the god's reputed lovers was that he himself was the god of just that age at which boys used to leave their mother's tutelage and live together. Their younger year-groups were subordinate to the older ones. They also attached themselves to individual older men. For boys as well as for girls this was the age of fugitive bloom. The tales represent Apollo's love, for a person of either sex, as having been very dangerous.[4]

If we carry his observations further, we begin to discern two kinds of man-to-man relationships. The image of Apollo with Admetus – where the relationship is *direct* – presents the archetypal background of adolescent initiation and, through the resemblance of Hyakinthos to the boy Apollo,[5] the invention of pederasty. The image of Hermes with Dryops gives a different picture, for the relationship was *indirect:* the story tells us that Hermes love was for the "Nymph of Dryops," a movement in and through fantasy

3. Kerényi, *The Gods of the Greeks, op. cit.,* p. 173.
4. *Ibid.,* p. 139.
5. *Ibid.,* p. 139.

(nymph). The outcome of this indirect relationship is the birth of a god – the great god Pan, a child of Hermes with the nymph of a mortal king.

These two images of Hermes and Apollo suggest relationships of importance for psychology. We can leave what the literature tells us about a god falling in love with a mortal, and turn to what this suggests psychologically: a relationship between two men ruled by the archetypal patterns of gods. We have the image of Hermes loving Dryops through a nymph and, in contrast, the image of Apollo loving Admetus directly. As my main concern in this chapter is with Hermes and the birth of Pan, I shall keep Apollo as a contrasting bas-relief to help us learn from these two models something about men's relationships.

In modern psychology, the conceptual frame has placed homosexuality within a sterile causalism that tries to understand it in terms of personal history. Undoubtedly psychology has seen homosexuality under the pressure imposed by Western culture's repression and has been unable to see it in relation to man's nature, his biology, expressed through the possibilities of the different archetypes. Thus an archetypal view of homo-erotica has been missed. Psychology's conceptual coinages are word-façades taken from 'scientific' fantasies but, in reality, they are a cover for a basic component in the history of Western culture. Without wishing to value-judge the scientific causalistic approach, it nevertheless occludes the perspective toward tracking down other archetypes that, during a lifetime, can take over men's relationships. Two of these archetypal situations are precisely our interest.

Recently there has been a changing attitude to eros among men and there have been attempts to modify the focus we have inherited. For example, we can read in *Time* how the Jesuits have tried to amend their rules and traditions among men of their Order: "Under the old rule of tactus, Jesuit seminarians were forbidden even to put an arm on the shoulder of a buddy; now they greet one another with warm *abrazos.*"[6]

There is no doubt it is of historical importance to reflect upon erotica among men. Some of its historicity has been worked out by D.P. Walker in his introduction to his book, *The Ancient Theology.*[7] There we see that the sudden repression of erotica among men in the early days of Christianity (St. Paul) is very much at the foundation of Western culture. Walker offers a mode for reflecting this repression, a repression that has become a seed of constant conflict at the core of our culture. It is a conflict we psychologists have to be aware of and deepen our insights into in order to be able to reflect from a deeper perspective and thus amend the jargon we have inherited in modern psychology. It is one thing to view homo-erotica as we have inherited it, and quite another to view it archetypally. These two views of homo-erotica (the inherited view and the archetypal view) obviously bring totally different results to psychotherapy. The psychological jargon applied to men's relationships – 'latent homosexuality,' 'negative mother complex,' 'transferential homosexuality,' etc. – has been too easily accepted, and the gods who are behind the struggle in which many men are involved remain undetected. The only inadequate recourse is to try by means of these clichés to 'control' this struggle introduced by the gods themselves.

If we want to improve our reading of the archetypes, we can hardly accept a psychotherapy which is biased toward man-to-man relationships, tending to see them only in terms of illness to be be cured or controlled. This attitude misplaces illness; and more importantly, it excludes the possibility of seeing through to the gods who, expressing aspects of nature, are behind these relationships. What appears in the personal picture as 'messes' are more likely frictions brought about by a peculiar mixing of the archetypes, the expression of a nature trying to hold itself

6. *Time,* April 23, 1973, "Cover Story."
7. Walker, *The Ancient Theology, op. cit.,* p. 8.

through what we call homosexuality. Seen in this way, psychotherapy could encourage psychic movement by following the dominant archetype in which erotica among men appears, and it would accept this dominant as the very vehicle for psychotherapeutic movement.

We have found two examples that offer more differentiated models for male relationships: the image of Hermes with Dryops in contrast with the homosexual pastoral relationship of Apollo with Admetus. Further archetypal patterns of men's relationships would appear in other mythological figures, e.g., Zeus and Ganymede.

But psychotherapy, apart from the conceptual jargon already mentioned, has done very little exploration of eros among men. In reading *The Freud/Jung Letters,*[8] we can hardly overlook the fact that the relationship between these two pioneers (and the group of men around them) had a strong missionary component.[9] They had found a common cause and, for a certain time, the relationship depended on the interests of their cause. But now, in this part of the century, we are aware that we have not inherited enough from these two geniuses of modern psychology and their man-to-man relationship to help us understand psychically what we are dealing with here. And this very lack is also part of the inheritance.

Moreover, if we look at the first meeting of these two pioneers in Vienna in 1909, in spite of Jung's hermetic nature, in this scene we have a picture of two men trying to gain power over each other.[10] Freud used his 'scientism' and

8. *The Freud/Jung Letters,* ed. William McGuire, trans. R. Manheim and R.F.C. Hull (London: Hogarth and Routledge & Kegan Paul, 1974).
9. Thanks to the gods, both Freud and Jung seem to have exhausted during the first half of life the appearance of missionarism in psychology. Evidently they needed the missionary component to 'hold' themselves in the early years of this century. Nowadays when a psychologist expresses himself at the missionary level, one feels it as a mockery and that the archetype is worn-out, exhausted.
10. Jung, *Memories, Dreams, Reflections, op. cit.,* p. 152; for Freud's reaction to the incident, see Appendix 1, pp. 333-34.

his discovery of the transference within a patriarchal fantasy. Jung exercised his power through occult phenomena. Their friendship shows few traces of having much relationship to each other's psyche. The relationship was based on building the pillars of modern psychology, through their common cause, case material, technique, and theory, but power intervened and ultimately destroyed their friendship.

Their relationship and conflict, union and separation, are the inheritance of their followers, and in the different analytical societies we can see a continuation of the same power-game. As the missionary drive has faded, the profession meets behind the façade of a Secret Society, a façade disguising the lack of psychic relationship. The internal conflicts have been accepted openly in terms of a power-game, while something as important as the lack of eros has not been denounced or even discussed.

The classic image of Hermes suggests the indirection of *falling in love with another man's fantasy:* the fantasy/erotica provided by the nymph. This could be the basis of what has been called a hermetic relationship between two men. This indirection, through a nymph, belonging to the archetypal realm of Hermes, is in contrast to Apollo's direct and idealized conception of love among men. Apollo's archetypal realm allows us to perceive homosexuality in terms of initiation during adolescence. We can also see the god behind regressions into this phase of adolescent initiation with its sometimes proselytizing Apollonic side. By means of the Apollonic perspective we can see through to the archetypal realm, the basic ground from which the erotica of the whole personality stems. The tale of Hermes with Dryops, however, enables us to see that this indirection in a man-to-man relationship brings its own result. This result is profoundly important for psychology and psychotherapy: the birth and epiphany of a god – Pan.

*
* *

Pan is a 'dead' god, and, though we do not worship him today, he is still present in all of us. His 'death' marked a change in the imagination of Western culture from the moment Plutarch[11] recorded the cry of lamentation that resounded when the classical world was shocked by the news: "Great Pan is dead." This news has often been considered a turning point in Western history, later leading to the legend of Pan dying in the moment Jesus Christ was mounted on the cross.

"Great Pan is dead" would have been a historical, factual death, a death pointing in the direction we have been implying, had it not been for another cry of lamentation. It is a cry challenging our sense of historicity, uttered in a time as historically extreme as the cry in Plutarch's time. It was a Victorian voice, the voice of an English poetess, that spoke when the fantasies of the theory of evolution were at their peak. By one of those historical curiosities she lived in London's Harley Street before it was taken over by the first wave of twentieth-century psychoanalysts and psychotherapists.

In her poem, "The Dead Pan," Elizabeth Barrett Browning wrote:

> Gods of Hellas, gods of Hellas,
> Can ye listen in your silence?
> Can your mystic voices tell us
> Where ye hide? In floating islands,
> With a wind that evermore
> Keeps you out of sight of shore?
> Pan, Pan is dead.

Her lamentation[12] does not tell of a missing link in the fog of evolution, but one missing in the history of Western

11. Plutarch, *Moralia,* 419 A-E.
12. I simply want to present the lamentation as it is and not try to 'analyze' the contents of the verse psychologically, e.g., "floating islands," "wind," and "out of sight of shore," as data from which Pan can be insighted as an autonomous complex.

culture: Pan as the missing link to the physical body. And more: it would be useless for psychology to hear in this verse an echo of the lament recorded by Plutarch, were it not for Jung's exploration and work on the collective unconscious that led him to tell the world and students of psychology that the ancient gods are not dead. On the contrary, they are very much alive in our unconscious, though, because of historical repression, they tend to appear at the core of our complexes, sometimes autonomously in neuroses and psychoses, and in physical illnesses.[13] In her lamentation, the English poetess expresses a dim awareness of the god Pan as an autonomous complex in a historical and geographical context seemingly far removed from the one in which the classical pagan gods manifested themselves.

These elements surrounding Pan – the cry recorded by Plutarch to Elizabeth Barrett Browning's lamentation – are part of the cultural legacy of Western man and can be included in our studies of psychology. This is possible as we have inherited Jung's theory of the unconscious, based on the historicity of the complexes and their pathology. However, at this point in the century we have more nourishing food which, as long as we bear in mind the pathological side of the gods, brings a reflection from another angle by showing the continuity of these so-called dead gods throughout the history of Western culture. Jean Seznec writes:

> In the preceding chapters we have studied in a general way the factors which determined the survival of the gods in the Middle Ages. The pagan divinities served as a vehicle for ideas so profound and so tenacious that it would have been impossible for them to perish.
>
> That being so, why do men too often speak of the "death of the gods" with the decline of the ancient world, and their "resurrection" in the dawn of the Italian Renaissance? We must remember that it was merely the content of the images of the

13. Jung, *CW* 13, para. 54.

gods which survived. The garment of the classical form had disappeared, having gradually been shed in favor of the wearers. And, in consequence, until our own day, history has failed to recognize them.[14]

But we psychotherapists cannot afford to fail to recognize them. The results in psychotherapy would be disastrous, knowing as we do that these gods carry complexes which appear in symptoms and illnesses. We should be indebted to the modern scholars, in particular to those connected with the Warburg Institute in London (Seznec, Yates, Wind, Panofsky, Saxl, Gombrich, Walker, etc.). Their work, with its emphasis on the Renaissance, offers new psychological food, stimulation and reflection. They offer us a scholarly research that has a more direct approach to the archetypes through their interest in images (the history of Western culture and its art).

The reflections that this scholarship transmits to us revitalize the spirit and feed the fantasy so that what might be going on in psychotherapy today, historically speaking, could be seen in terms of a new renascence (Renaissance), perhaps psychotherapy's greatest chance. These scholars are concerned solely with the roots of Western culture, with the North/South conflict, a conflict in every Western soul. They are not occupied with the East as were many scholars in the early part of the century, an interest that led to studies on comparative symbolism and comparative religion. That scholarship had an immense influence on Jung's generation and still serves – to the neglect of Western cultural imagery – as the basic curriculum for learning the amplificatory method used in Jungian psychology.

Furthermore, the work of the modern scholars gives us the feeling that the archetypes of the collective unconscious are not so remote. If the archetypes are considered from the ego point of view and the insights are symbolical, then, of

14. Seznec, *The Survival of the Pagan Gods,* trans. B.F. Sessions, *op. cit.,* p. 149.

course, the result is a sense of remoteness. But modern scholarship has shrunk this distance by retraining the psyche to read the image. We are offered a new hermeneutic which can refresh the study of psychology, enabling us to remain within the complexities and constancies of Western culture when approaching archetypal images as they appear in psychotherapy.

The school in Zurich has its own approach to the appearance in the psyche of this strange god, Pan. Discussion and interpretation of him in dreams and paintings are part of Jungian studies. Although no archetype can be thought of in terms of a standard work, a basic interpretative text, this is most evident in the case of Pan. The relation to this god depends particularly upon each analyst's complexes, history, and attitude, and how the pathology (complexes and history) of the patient expresses Pan's appearance in psychotherapy. Pan is the god of panic, and it is in this manifestation of his pathology that Pan can panic both analyst and patient. Panic in the analytical situation can either be of value within the spectrum of a healing epiphany of this god, or can become uncontrollable, bringing misunderstanding, and at worst, catastrophic results.

Pan creates most panic when his image is presented under the historical disguise of the devil. With this sort of appearance in psychotherapy, there is only a very slight possibility of reverting to the image of the "God of Hellas" as seen by the English poetess. In the longing expressed through the imagery of her poem, she may have been able to hold her madness by reviving the image of Pan as a true god, and not merely as one side of the split between god and the devil.[15] (We have to remember that throughout Manichean Christianity Pan alone has carried the 'shadow of God.')

Pan is the god of nightmare and epilepsy, and the discovery of masturbation[16] was attributed to him. When reacting to a patient's nightmare, there is a difference between trying to analyze it and accepting it as the epiphany of a god under one of his surnames, Ephialtes.[17] Pan's connection to epilepsy points to the possibilities of research into a psychotherapy of this 'mal,' of opening the continent of the physical body for an exploration which aims to improve the equilibrium in this illness; or, to put it mythologically – to make a more favorable connection to the god who was conceived as being at the origin of the illness.

As the discoverer of masturbation, Pan gives a frame of reference for the whole gamut of masturbatory fantasies, from the most extreme obsessive-compulsive ones to those that bring a relationship to the body; from Pan's destructive appearance as an autonomous complex – as the 'Devil' history has taught us to reject – to the possibility of connecting imaginatively to the different gods and goddesses. (In masturbation itself, all the possibilities are there for connecting to the archetypes.) Here I would like to go further and suggest that, through masturbatory fantasies, the repeated sexual image – reflecting the part of man's nature which does not change[18] – can either be accepted, thereby bringing a deeper insight into the personality, or can continue obsessively with no insight. Moreover, masturbation is the field where new sexual imagery first occurs. Within the struggle with masturbation, the appearance of these new images – the part of man's nature which moves – enables the self-detection of new psychic movers. But this is not all.

15. A different view of the compensatory function of Pan is offered by Edgar Wind:

In the ever-changing *balance des dieux* the gods reveal their Protean nature: but the very fact that each god contains his opposite in himself, and can change into it when occasion demands, makes him shadow forth the nature of Pan in whom all opposites are one.

Pagan Mysteries in the Renaissance, Chapter XIII, "Pan and Proteus" (Penguin: Harmondsworth, 1967), p. 199.

16. Hillman, "An Essay on Pan" in *Pan and the Nightmare* (New York and Zurich: Spring Publications, 1972), p. xxxii. For his fuller reflections upon masturbation see "Toward the Archetypal Model of the Masturbation Inhibition" (1966) in *Loose Ends, op. cit.*

17. W.H. Roscher, *"Ephialtes:* A Pathological-Mythological Treatise on the Nightmare in Classical Antiquity," in *Pan and the Nightmare* (New York and Zurich: Spring Publications, 1972).

Though it may seem an awkward way, masturbation offers the possibility of making a self-diagnosis of one's psychological state and illness by becoming more precise about what fantasies are at work in one's actual psychological movement. Masturbation has been seen mostly from perspectives far removed from the archetypal sphere of Pan. In any case, there is no denying that masturbation is the sexuality attributed to this son of Hermes, and that Pan rules the physical body of our psyche. Masturbation is the basic sexuality and one of nature's wonders, for it at once connects man's sexual images and his physical and emotional body. When there is masturbation in a dream, it is an epiphany of Pan, expressing the psychic need to recognize and accept what has been most repressed by Christianity: basic sexuality and the emotional body. One has to recognize masturbation from within this complexity. After two millennia of repression, masturbation, which had its place in the great mythologies of ancient times, has reappeared in this century's literature: James Joyce brought masturbation and masturbatory fantasies and imagery into *Ulysses*. This can be seen as an example of the revival of a pagan god in the psyche of a twentieth-century man.

To go on with our theme of Pan and pathology, we see that he is able to carry the lunatic, as shown by the image of Pan carrying Selene.[19] This image suggests that the answer of Pan's psychology to the lunatic aspect of the psyche is

18. The idea of human nature having two parts – a part that does not change and a part that moves – is valuable for psychotherapy. My thoughts regarding this idea were stimulated first by the Spanish poet, Antonio Machado in his book, *Juan de Mairena*. Later I found similar ideas in *Hermetica*, trans. Walter Scott (London: Dawson, 1968), Libellus II, p. 135f., in the discussion between Hermes Trismegistus and Asclepius. Although in another chapter of this book I discuss these two parts in an easier fashion, let me put in a nutshell my thoughts in this respect. It is of obvious practical value in psychotherapy to have an awareness of these two elements, so that we can detect what in human nature does not change, so as to localize our psychotherapeutic aims in that part which moves.

19. Virgil, *Georgica*, 3.391.

simply to carry it. Needless to say the implication is that it is Pan in us who carries our lunacy. Among his nymph-fantasies, Echo was the most beloved, who, in having no physical existence, seems to provide the most intimate element in Pan: and it is in Echo that Pan reflects the instinctual essence of his godhead. Pan and Echo are complementary. Pan's echoes have a repercussion in the soul, making the soul at Pan's body level.

The association of Pan and Echo leads into another myth, that of Narcissus, who, in fleeing from Pan's Echo (and therefore rejecting Pan), began an infatuation with his own image and became what is called today 'an acute or chronic psychotic case.' In another tale, that of Eros and Psyche recorded by Apuleius, Pan and Echo were nearby on the riverbank when Psyche wanted to kill herself. This tale, in a very subtle way, tells us that they rescued her from this suicidal attempt. So the classical myths remind us of two sides of Pan's Echo: that of making Narcissus mad, and that of helping to rescue Psyche. These two sides of Echo, one showing pathology and the other a psychotherapy, have reappeared in this century in what we could call the 'echo conditions' of the psyche.

Eugen Bleuler[20] described echolalia and echopraxia as secondary symptoms of schizophrenia. The genius of an American psychotherapist, Carl Rogers, introduced Echo, the nymph of Pan, son of Hermes, as a method into his psychotherapeutic practice. Here we have two pictures belonging to this century's psychology: a psychiatrist who diagnosed a condition; and a psychotherapist who, without diagnosing, therapeutically approached the psyche – through a personal hunch and probably unaware of its archetypal background – with the very instrument diagnosed by the psychiatrist as a secondary symptom. These pictures are worth keeping in mind as they so clearly present two aspects of psychotherapy, two different approaches to

20. Eugen Bleuler, *Lehrbuch der Psychiatrie,* 9 Aufl. (Berlin: Springer Verlag, 1955), p. 92.

illness. On the one hand, there is always the psychiatric-diagnostic approach and, on the other, there is the therapeutic approach through Pan. Together they have provided me with a historical reference to frame my own experience and insights into a psychotherapy constellated by Pan.[21]

The 'happening' of Pan's echo in psychotherapy can constellate a true epiphany of Pan, which is one of the most vivid expressions of the psychotherapeutic relationship. Like cures like, *Similis similibus curantur.*[22] This is where the real symmetry happens, where the dance is, where the psychotherapy of Pan is. It is the expression of two bodies dancing in unison, a psychotherapy of the body. When this happens we can be sure we are in the realm where Pan appears in a psychotherapy through body movements, within a sort of dance, constellating the transference which belongs to him.[23]

The analyst is challenged when the patient's imagery involves archetypes that are outside the archetypal realms with which he or she is familiar. This presents a difficulty in finding an attitude akin to the patient's archetypal background. The work of modern scholars on rhetoric,[24] the

21. My own therapeutic experience of Echo happened more through Bleuler's small reference than Roger's about whom, at the time, I knew nothing.
22. I had a patient who confessed that at last her madness had a companion. We discussed the difference between madness accompanied and madness in solitude. Most of the therapy had been based on echo reflection.
23. I appreciate that, in the first edition, this passage stimulated Joan Chodorow, a dance therapist, in her practice; see her paper "Dance/ Movement and Body Experience in Analysis" in *Jungian Analysis,* ed. Murray Stein (Open Court: La Salle, 1982). Actually, I wrote this passage as a result of my experience at the dancing parties I led at the Zurichberg Clinic when I worked there.
24. Yates, *The Art of Memory, op. cit.*; for the rediscovery of Hermogenes see her *Giordano Bruno and the Hermetic Tradition* (London: Routledge and Kegan Paul, 1964). In 1970/71 a seminar on the Picatrix was held at Spring Publications. The vivid happenings during this seminar gave a training and insight into the emotions and expressions of the different planets (archetypes), their imagery, talismans, etc.

different styles of rhetoric as a way to connect to the different archetypes, could be of great help in this direction. We need to know more about archetypal rhetoric and to train ourselves in this. In my discussion of a Pan psychotherapy, it seems to me I have been referring to the 'rhetoric of Pan': Echo, who connects us to the constellation of Pan in psychotherapy.

Jungian analysis has yet to explore a psychotherapy based on the archetypal constellation brought by the patient, and to be acquainted with the classical conception of rhetoric, talismanic medicine, the different ways of connecting to the different gods – the constellations of the different archetypes. These are very old ideas, but they are still waiting to be developed by modern psychotherapy. And, in spite of the fact that Jungian psychology has opened many new doors for psychotherapy, analytical work is mainly conducted through discussion of dreams, paintings, and active imagination, mostly by way of amplifying symbols. So if Pan appears in a dream or painting, bringing with his image an expression of the patient's unconscious demand, the discussion continues with more or less the same attitude. Because Pan has not been allowed to appear with his own rhetoric or style, the interpretation of 'Pan material' is invariably based on the 'devilish' aspect of this god and so the patient is 'warned' of the dangers inherent in Pan. As yet no psychotherapy exists which pays attention to the essential reality that each god (or goddess) needs a different ritual, a different cult, and a living rhetoric.

*
* *

Let us return to the image of Pan's birth as told in the *Homeric Hymn to Pan,* keeping to and reflecting from that image. I have suggested that Pan was born of a relationship between two men through their fantasy (nymph). The indirection of this nymphic third can turn a relationship into a threesome situation. The possible repercussions of such a threesome in a man's soul can scarcely be understood conceptually. But as hermetic relationships they bring their own possibilities for psychotherapy. Moreover, they bring a different model for therapy itself, i.e., a man-to-man relationship through a nymph resulting in Pan, a god, on whose ground healing can happen. Because the appearance of Pan/Echo in psychotherapy is in itself a repercussion, our understanding here must be determined by the very constellation we are trying to understand. For I do not want to pretend that we can grasp what is going on from a perspective outside the Pan constellation.

Because psychological interpretations about Pan have followed the Christian tradition and strongly painted him with the colors of the devil, these interpretations tend to fall into discussions about evil, so here I would like to discuss Pan in terms of the psychodynamic of compensation. The compensatory function of the psyche, discovered by Jung in 1907 and which established the modern psychodynamic view of the psyche, is important for our discussion of Pan. In one of his passages on compensation, Jung writes:

> The psyche is a self-regulating system that maintains its equilibrium just as the body does. Every process that goes too far immediately and inevitably calls forth compensations, and without these there would be neither a normal metabolism nor a normal psyche. In this sense we can take the theory of compensation as a basic law of psychic behavior. Too little on one side results in too much on the other. Similarly, the relation between conscious and unconscious is compensatory.[25]

Pan was at the center of the repression of the pagan gods, just as he was at the center of the longing for compensation expressed in the poem of the English poetess. It seems that Pan, in terms of the function of compensation, represents an extreme possibility for the psyche to find either a natural

25. Jung, *Modern Man in Search of a Soul*, trans. W.S. Dell & C.F. Baynes (London: Kegan, Paul, 1933), *op. cit.*, para. 20.

self-regulation or enter into madness. But here I would like to stress that it is one thing to have enough awareness to keep an eye on the compensatory function of the psyche with its natural 'self-regulation,' and quite another to accept into psychotherapy the *image* of Pan. I do not want to say explicitly that modern psychotherapy's theoretical compensatory/complementary approach to Pan tends to constellate the panic side of him, though there is no doubt that, historically, psychic compensation has its validity in the psyche. Nevertheless, as I have worked out, Pan's appearance in psychotherapy calls for a quite different response: a response coming from Pan in the analyst, a consciousness that includes Pan's healing function, his rhetoric, Echo, and the symmetric dance.

For those who prefer to live a psychotherapy more on the lines of the epiphany of the gods and the archetypes, a basic knowledge of, and feeling for Who's Who in mythology is needed. In the case of Pan, owing to the particular pathologies attributed to him, a historical perspective is essential: that in Christianity, through repression, Pan and the complexes around him became equated with evil and the imagery of the devil. (It is interesting to note that a later Greek tradition tells us that in Hellas there were devils too, 'evildoers'[26] – but these were Titans with souls made of iron and steel.) In Greek classical times neither Pan, nor the chthonic gods of his kind, ever carried a projection even remotely akin to the Christian one. Though, needless to say, all the gods and goddesses each have their own style of destruction.

The aim of this chapter has been to introduce the imagery of Pan's birth and epiphany into psychotherapy and to discuss his image from the viewpoint of a psychology of the archetypes. I particularly wished to stress the fact that Pan's birth was made possible by two men loving each other through a nymph. The insight that Pan is concerned with

26. Kerényi, *Gods of the Greeks, op. cit.*, p. 208.

the psychotherapy of the body can open a door for a psychotherapeutic approach to the pathologies attributed to him. It can offer, also, a psychotherapeutic approach to the analytical situation in which the patient's homosexuality appears center-stage. Instead of a homosexuality with no psychological body, this approach could provide that same homosexuality with the body psychology of Pan, son of Hermes.

Chapter V

Hermes Chasing a Nymph

There are three classical tales of Hermes with the nymphs, and I would like to consider them as three variations on a theme. By moving in this direction, we are coming closer to Hermes' mother's side: "Of all the gods Hermes was the only nymph's son who had a permanent place on Olympus…"[1] Hermes was closely associated with the nymphs and, probably, he is the only one who really knows what underlies the word 'nymph.'

In this book, we are limiting ourselves to the classical image, so let us look at the word 'nymph' as an image in itself. Also, let us not confuse the classical image of the nymph with any seemingly similar elements such as can be found in literature or fairy tales. The three tales we are going to be concerned with in this chapter are tales from classical mythology, in which gods and goddesses play their roles, thus giving a psychical consistency that fairy tales do not have. Neither would I like us to associate the nymph with the Jungian concept of the anima, because that would be to fall into the entanglements of her many presentations, "her always changeable veils." Jung's followers have seen the nymph as a "spirit of nature,"[2] but this association offers little differentiation, giving to the nymph a vaporous ethereal connotation which lacks the consistency of the archetypal connection which is our interest. In psychology, we

---

1. Kerényi, *The Gods and the Greeks, op. cit.,* p. 177.
2. Emma Jung, *Animus and Anima* (Spring Publications: Zurich and London, 1974), p. 50.

refer everything to man's nature, yet we tend to forget that we are, in fact, a part of nature. Probably the use of the word 'spirit' reinforces this illusion. The anima has been seen by Jung and his followers as an archetype, and although it is admissible that the nymph forms part of the "embodiment of the anima,"[3] nevertheless I prefer to discuss her in relation to her classical image. So let us keep to the nymph as she was portrayed in classical mythology and the legacy of art. I am basically interested in what she can specifically tell the psyche through the stories about her in classical mythology.

In Jungian psychology, there seems to be some confusion between the nymph and the anima. The anima tends to have absorbed elements of the feminine which for psychotherapy could be more precisely defined. If we try to see the imagery of the nymph from the Jungian point of view, we cannot connect to the specific images of the nymph which mythology offers us and the analogies they provoke. The anima has been seen as an element which, within its many complexities, has to be redeemed and integrated as one of the goals of the individuation process. Her role is to lead into the analytical process of individuation through a revelation of constant and endless conflicts.[4] The picture of the nymph is quite different. We know that Hermes is not a hero; so we have to think of the nymph, because of her close association with him, as having nothing to do with heroism or redemption but as associated with the undignified side of life,[5] an aspect of Hermes discussed in Chapter I. The idea of the redemption of the anima comes from the way in

3. *Ibid.*, p. 46.
4. I do not want to extend my thoughts about the anima here. The reader must be well-acquainted with the profuse literature on this theme. Most of the discussion is concerned with her phenomenological appearance, a standpoint rather distant from where the anima functions. Certainly the anima as the companion of the soul, as a living connection to the emotions, belongs to man's inner and secret side. As Jung said, it is the inner man that Christianity has betrayed and that modern psychology wants to 'deal' with, but does not know how.

which the feminine and the anima are insighted by other archetypes, but not from within a Hermes view.

To see the anima as the *imago* of the feminine only in men is inadequate since, in being archetypal, it is present in both men and women. Recently some Jungians have become more inclined to accept this evidence and even provide a quantitative aspect for an approach to the anima: This man has more anima than another, or this woman is more anima than another. It is an approach that is part of the inheritance of Jungian thought. Another approach, at a different level, would be to say: This man has more femininity than another, and this woman is more feminine than another. This latter approach is more a reading of the other's body as an image.

Kerényi writes: "The word *numphe* meant a female being through whom a man became the *numphios,* i.e., the happy bridegroom who had fulfilled the purpose of his manhood."[6] Here, Kerényi brings a hint in terms of initiation, a preview of the initiatory side of the nymphs. Later on, we shall have a picture of this in their rearing of Aeneas. I quote the etymological connections of Kerényi as a coloring through which to enrich our attempt to stick to the imagery of the nymphs. After hinting at the initiatory aspect, he introduces the pathological connection when he says:

> In our language *numpholeptus,* "one seized by the nymphs," was the word for what the Latins called a *lymphaticus* – a term in which *lympha* is a rendering of "nymph," but in the sense of "water" – or *lunaticus,* "moon-sick," which was a later word for a person who became crazy from time to time, or only slightly, and was regarded as a victim of the nymphs.[7]

---

5. We have to give the nymph her own place in the psychology of Hermes. To generalize would be fatal. I want both to differentiate her and to stress her importance. Here we can recall the nymph Salmacis, who contributed to the creation of the Hermaphrodite, with its importance for psychology.

6. Kerényi, *The Gods of the Greeks, op. cit.,* p. 177.

7. *Ibid.,* p. 179.

Though there were nymphs of trees and groves, the word
'nymph' is, evidently, associated etymologically with the
element of water, bringing with it a group of images related
to this element. Kerényi also says: "The term could be
applied to a great goddess as well as to a mortal maiden."[8]
Kerényi stresses the evident archetypal connection of the
nymph and makes her initiatory side more explicit. Probably just as all the gods were also children, the goddesses had
to endure some time as nymphs (nymphets).

According to the classic Jungian approach you could say
that Hermes, in being the son of a nymph and in his chasing
of nymphs, was possessed by the mother complex and the
anima: the complexes of his history. However, in saying this,
there is no image and we risk falling into psychological
preconceptions. It is not my intention here to be in conflict
with Jungian psychology. I merely want to keep to the image
side, and only mention in passing any possible conflict with
the conceptual side. I am interested in reading the image as
an archetypal picture of life and, for this, using a concept
does not help.

Homer, in the *Iliad,* tells the first tale on our theme of
Hermes and the nymphs. It is the story of Polymele, daughter of Pylas, an unmarried girl:

> She was a beautiful dancer, and the great god Hermes the
> Giant-killer had fallen in love with her when she caught his eye
> as she was playing her part in the choir of Artemis of the
> Golden Distaff, the goddess of the chase. The gracious Hermes
> took her straight to her bedroom unobserved, lay in her arms,
> and made her the mother of a splendid child destined, as
> Eudorus, to be a great runner and man of war. When in due
> course the baby had been brought into the world by Eileithyia,
> the goddess of travail, and had opened his eyes to the sun, a
> powerful chieftain, Echecles, son of Actor, married the
> mother, for whom he paid an ample dowry, and took her home
> with him, while Eudorus was carefully looked after and brought

8. *Ibid.,* p. 177.

up by his old grandfather, Phylas, who could have shown him no greater devotion had he been his own son.[9]

It seems that Polymele was a nymph in the retinue of Artemis and, of course, a virgin. This tale gives a hint of a first differentiation of what is rather a puzzle: the difference between being in the retinue of a goddess and being the child of a goddess. Artemis, for example, being a virgin, has no children but a retinue of companions and nymphs, which could be insighted as pointing to the initiatory side of the goddess. To be the child of a god or goddess is quite another thing. For instance, Hippolytus is a classical example of being a 'child' of Artemis, and his fate, as told in Euripides' *Hippolytus,* was a direct result of this.

Polymele's love affair with Hermes is our first variation in the Hermes/nymph relationship. Here we can begin to use two terms in connection with Hermes that I shall try to develop later. Otto presents him as the god of love by chance,[10] what might be called 'cheap sexuality.' This notion combines the classical image with the modern social, psychological, and moral ideas of love by chance (cheap sexuality). The tale tells us that a child, conceived out of this love by chance, is the product of an archetypal genealogy, without the derogatory connotation of illegitimacy.

Homer's tale neatly recounts a situation that was lived in pagan times within the grace of its own history. Classical writers told of this sort of situation many times, of a god or goddess as one parental side of a mortal's begetting. Homer tells the story of a life situation in which the psychology of one parental image is attributed to a god, Hermes. To attribute one's genealogy to a god or goddess leaves an imprint and marks the meaning of a whole life. However, once history and culture became dominated by the concretization of direct parental genealogy, owing to the pressure of the fantasy of the one God, this imprint faded. Thus the

9. Homer, *The Iliad,* Rieu. trans., *op. cit.,* p. 297.
10. Otto, *The Homeric Gods, op. cit.,* p. 111.

gods' and goddesses' genealogy passed into the 'collective unconscious.' But the unconscious is precisely the realm of Jungian psychology, the realm in which psychology has to search. Psychotherapy has inherited the stress on concretized genealogy. The limitation of a concretized personal genealogy can compress the personality. We can see that psychotherapy has been overburdened by the literalized aspect of the conflicts and traumas of the family complex. So, while accepting this kind of reality, we can also try to detect the underlying archetypal genealogy of the patient. This approach provides two possibilities. Firstly, the patient is released in some measure from the pressures of the personal genealogy, and secondly, a new or unexpected course in psychotherapy and life is propitiated.

In our study of Hermes, I have returned repeatedly to the idea of the children of the gods, an idea developed in Jean Seznec's *The Survival of the Pagan Gods*.[11] However, I want to move his work on the old tradition of the "children of the planets," in which he traces the astrological appearance and hidden iconography of pagan images within Christianity, in a more psychotherapeutic direction. As classical imagery is the basis of this study, I want to read therein its provision of a similar idea, which would be the children of the archetypes. The idea is to return to the classical images of the children of the gods as they were imagined before these images became confused and difficult to detect, because of the contamination and conflict of Western history. We need to improve our reading of the classical image in order to arrive at a genealogy more fitting for psychotherapy; to move away from the suffocation of concretized personal genealogy, and to refresh psychotherapy with a genealogy more suited to the psychological personality of the patient. For this we must train ourselves to search out the archetypal form of life given for, and by, the patient's psyche. We must discover this other genealogy of the gods and goddesses, of which the patient is a child, and thus open the way for

11. Seznec, *The Survival of the Pagan Gods, op. cit.,* pp. 70ff.

psychic movement within the range of the given archetypal possibilities. We need to train ourselves in a reading of the archetypes similar to that Renaissance legacy of being aware of the gods and the archetypal situation behind their images. In this last connection I would like to mention two paintings by Velasquez which provide a handy example of what I am trying to discuss: the epiphany of a god, Vulcan, in a blacksmith's forge, "Vulcan's Forge," and the presence of Bacchus seen in the faces of the drinkers in "The Drunkards."

Homer's tale of Polymele gives, in just a few lines, the image of a life situation which in those times was connected with a god, and, with this acceptance of the god, the outcome is more psychological, more human, if you will. The end of the story goes beyond the most farfetched happy ending of a Hollywood film, long before Hollywood ever existed, and has a more focused psychological retina than the happiest fairy-tale ending of a rose-petalled novel, thanks to the intervention of the genealogy of the gods.

*
* *

The second variation on our theme as told in the *Homeric Hymn to Aphrodite* is more subtle in that the motif of Hermes and the nymph is conveyed indirectly, a tale within a tale. Aphrodite introduces a woman's fantasy, 'telling a tale,' maintaining that psychological feminine borderline between a lie and a fantasy in order to bring about her love-affair with Anchises.

Zeus arranged that Aphrodite be filled with "sweet desire to be joined in love with a mortal man... And so he put in her heart sweet desire for Anchises..."[12] After she had beautified herself, Aphrodite approached Anchises not as a goddess but as the daughter of a mortal, Otreus. Then she

12. "The Homeric Hymn to Aphrodite," in *Hesiod, The Homeric Hymns and Homerica, op. cit.,* p. 415.

goes on to fantasize, introducing herself as a maiden in Artemis' retinue:

> "And now the Slayer of Argus with the golden wand has caught me up from the dance of huntress Artemis, her with the golden arrows. For there were many of us, nymphs and marriageable maidens, playing together; and an innumerable company encircled us: from these the Slayer of Argus with the golden wand rapt me away. He carried me over many fields of mortal men and over land untilled and unpossessed, where savage wild-beasts roam through shady coombes, until I thought never again to touch the life-giving earth with my feet. And he said that I should be called the wedded wife of Anchises, and should bear you goodly children."[13]

This image probably expresses a constant in woman's psyche: how, through the delicacy and indirection of her fantasy, she transmits her desire to a man – fantasies and desires backed by the god who archetypally carries sexual fantasy. She entices Anchises with the fantasy, or lie, of presenting herself as an innocent virginal girl who has been carried off by Hermes. And here we may introduce the fantasy of rape as being part of woman's enticement of a man. Aphrodite's fantasy conveys an image of Hermes chasing a nymph, catching and 'raping' her,[14] but this is seen from the feminine point of view. Aphrodite's desire was fulfilled and resulted in the conception of a son, Aeneas, who became an important hero in the history of Western culture.

The hymn tells us that after Aeneas' conception out of a love-affair based on Aphrodite's 'tale' of being a mortal maiden – her Hermes/nymph fantasy – the goddess reveals herself as goddess, which, of course, ends the 'human' love-

---

13. *Ibid.*, p. 415.
14. Chasing, catching, and rape seem to imply three different levels of sexual fantasy. Depth psychology has not differentiated these fantasies, or at least only in the branch of psychology which deals with legal and criminal psychiatry.

affair. Her first reaction is one of feminine shame and she accuses Anchises:

> "And now because of you I shall have great shame among the deathless gods henceforth, continually. For until now they feared my jibes and the wiles by which, or soon, or late, I mated all the immortals with mortal women, making them all subject to my will. But now my mouth shall no more have this power among the gods; for very great has been my madness, my miserable and dreadful madness, and I went astray out of my mind who have gotten a child beneath my girdle, mating with a mortal man."[15]

Aphrodite's strong expression of her shame gives us a beautiful picture of a woman's reaction to a love-affair she considers to be undignified and beneath her. Zeus caused Aphrodite to become infatuated with a mortal. Then Aphrodite told her story of Hermes chasing a nymph to entice Anchises into the love-affair. Evidently the image of Hermes chasing a nymph and the rape touched Anchises' psyche deeply and moved him into love. After the *copula* and conception she came to her senses (so to speak) and all her goddess-pride expresses her disgust over her desire for a mortal. She has awakened from the sexual fantasy plotted by Zeus, with the help of Hermes. The tale gives us the opportunity to take a look at the archetypal background of a woman's love-affair with a man who is 'inferior' to her. In this story, the asymmetry in the relationship is presented in the form of a relationship between a goddess and a mortal. If we look at this kind of asymmetry in terms of life, it is a relationship between a woman of pronounced characteristics (archetypally well-defined) with a man much less so (archetypally vague). This kind of relationship has been dealt with psychotherapeutically more as a pathology. It has been seen causalistically in terms of transference to the concrete father; the father *imago* is so positive that she has to

---

15. "The Homeric Hymn to Aphrodite," *op. cit.*, p. 423.

find an inferior lover, who cannot match up to her father; the father complex takes over the personality and expresses itself through a love-affair. Now the classic tale implies there are archetypes involved in such a situation/complex, which, if it repeats itself too often, can bring a woman into psychotherapy.

Now if we look at this image of goddess-woman/mortal-man again, we can begin to see that it gives us a further field of insight for psychotherapy. Here, I want to introduce the psychology of the consort, in which the woman of pronounced characteristics plays an active role and procures the love-affair by way of her own fantasies, and the man remains rather passive and falls into the 'love plot.' In reading the archetypal situation portrayed in the story, we are perhaps dealing in another way with the same elements which have appeared in psychology under the jargon of the 'strong' woman and the 'weak' man. And we can conceive this asymmetric relationship between a strong, well-defined woman and a less defined man, in terms of consort psychology, particularly when it is 'accepted' and lived throughout a long lifetime with all the ups and downs and the conflicts of such an asymmetry.

Moreover, in looking at the elements provided by the tale with our attention focused on the motif we are concerned with – Hermes chasing a nymph – we can speculate that perhaps the link holding this relationship together is this very fantasy of Hermes chasing a nymph. The fantasy provides the archetypal elements – a nymph in the retinue of Artemis, chased and raped by Hermes – that give to such a relationship its container. Though in ordinary life, what in Aphrodite was an immediate reaction, often becomes the monotony of a constant nagging.

There is another image in the continuation of the story which complements the idea of consort psychology which I am trying to formulate. It is when Aphrodite instructs Anchises in this way:

"And if any mortal man asks you who got your dear son beneath her girdle, remember to tell him as I bid you: say he is the offspring of one of the flower-like nymphs who inhabit this forest-clad hill. But if you tell all and foolishly boast that you lay with rich-crowned Aphrodite, Zeus will smite you in his anger with a smoking thunderbolt."[16]

Throughout, the love-affair and the resulting child (Aeneas) are kept within the Hermes/nymph fantasy which, I would like to stress, is an essential ingredient in the psychology of the consort. Though, in literature, Aeneas is always known as the child of Aphrodite and Anchises, nevertheless the tale shows that, as far as Aphrodite was concerned, he was conceived by a nymph, a virgin in the retinue of Artemis, who was chased and raped by Hermes.

Homer depicts Aeneas as one of the best men of Troy. And Virgil, taking him as a model for the hero, conqueror, and founder, conceived Aeneas, though he was a child of Aphrodite and Anchises, a child of consort psychology, as having such a bond with his father that it can be taken as a model for the son/father relationship, a model of therapeutic value. Virgil tells of Aeneas carrying his father on his shoulders out of the sack of Troy, the father who perhaps weighs all the more because he is a consort father. Later, during his career as a true hero, Aeneas was able to fulfill another important task of the hero; he went down into the underworld to visit his father. In actual fact, this is not an image of heroic glory; on the contrary, it is tinted with the painful side of life's complexes, for Dido, also, was in the underworld. In any event, our insight is deepened into a son/father relationship which, to me, is one of the most psychological. Nevertheless, Aeneas was a child of Aphrodite in terms of consort psychology: the mother well-defined by social class, money, intellect, education, etc., whereas the father remains archetypally vague. Aphrodite's fantasy of Hermes chasing a nymph was at the center of the concep-

16. *Ibid.*, p. 425.

tion of Aeneas. It was the hermetic element which procured his birth.

Just before Aphrodite's final instructions to Anchises quoted above, she gives us another image of Hermes and the nymphs when she describes the place where her son is to be brought up. Is it a place of initiation?

> "As for the child, as soon as he sees the light of the sun, the deep-breasted mountain nymphs who inhabit this great and holy mountain shall bring him up. They rank neither with mortals nor with immortals: long indeed do they live, eating heavenly food and treading the lovely dance among the immortals, and with them the Sileni and the sharp-eyed Slayer of Argus mate in the depths of pleasant caves..."[17]

This image of the place chosen by Aphrodite for the upbringing and initiation of her son takes us to a realm of fantasy, an erotic Aphroditic fantasy, where the image is at its most psychic. The setting is so psychic that it defies any attempt to discuss it. The image contains a completely psychic expression of the place, the *locus,* where this archetype is enacted: "a dance among the immortals," with a Dionysian touch due to the presence of the Sileni. The bucolic beauty of this image has touched the souls of many image-makers in our culture who have left us their tribute to this soul-making theme.

The image induces us to think in terms of symmetry: the nymphs with Hermes and the Sileni. They dance (there is no dance that is not symmetric), and there is mating "in the depths of pleasant caves." There is neither a man chasing a woman (Hermes chasing a nymph), nor a woman expressing desire for a man by using the metaphor of the chase (Aphrodite's fantasy of being chased by Hermes). We can see no asymmetrical relationship from either the masculine or the feminine side.

This is the environment in which Aeneas, the son of Aphrodite and Anchises, was to be brought up, a place

17. *Ibid.,* p. 425.

where sexual fantasy has its own setting. Growing up, archetypally speaking, is to be initiated, and as this image implies, to be initiated into sexual fantasies. But this has nothing to do with the impressions we have gathered from psychologists and psychiatrists in this respect, the illusion of initiating children into sexuality through a 'mass' sexual education, scientific and explanatory. This is an approach which destroys each child's personal curiosity and the mysteries of sexual imagination, and marks an overt lack of taste and disrespect for the child. This approach fails to see that of course the child has sexuality, the sexuality of the dominant archetype of its nature and personality. Perhaps there are children that need more initiation into sexuality than others, but this has nothing to do with 'mass' education into sexuality. Each child has to 'educate' itself sexually, and to live the sexuality of the archetype it is a child of. There are no preconceived models and, as was discussed earlier, each archetype has its own sexuality.

If we look at the image – Hermes, the Sileni, and the dance of the nymphs – from the manic side, and include the elements we have already mentioned of 'love by chance' and 'cheap sexuality,' we can see we are in tune with what our scholars said. Hermes is the god of sexuality, including cheap sexuality and love by chance. This kind of sexuality has been seen by most students of psychology only from the compulsive and manic side. So-called manic sexuality could be said to express a paralyzation in, or a lacking of, one of the steps of initiation, or a distortion of it. The possibility of manic sexuality being a psychic mover has not yet been realized.

From my viewpoint of a psychology of the archetypes, I would like to discuss something which I find questionable. To what extent is sexual mania a condition requiring treatment? Does keeping it within these terms prevent the actual realm of psychotherapy in these cases from being seen? Psychotherapy should serve the soul-making process and respect a sexuality which has its own god, its own archetypal form, behind it. Here we have another legacy of this century's psychology, which has insisted on viewing this behavior as a sickness requiring treatment and has tended to base it causalistically in the parental situation (concrete genealogy). The treatment of mania, nymphomania, has been carried out in relation to the patient's childhood and parental dependency. The archetypes involved have not been seen, and therefore the patient's nature is not seen either, and a possible psychic movement, despite the mania of that nymph (the nymph-patient), is not procured.

It is one thing to see this kind of situation – all its elements of compulsion, family background, and social conflict – solely in conflictive terms as if no archetypes were there, and quite another to see through to the archetype behind it. A cooling down of the conflictive aspect depends on the analyst's perception of the archetype involved. If this imagery is constellated in analysis – the archetypal fantasy we all have of Hermes chasing a nymph – through its own epiphany (love by chance and cheap sexuality), it also moves the psyche. If the analyst insists upon seeing it within the legacy of modern psychology, as a problem located in the parental situation, he is pushed into the role of trying to control the situation. Consequently, he evades seeing through to the archetypal background and lacks respect for a nature which expresses itself in this way. Both analyst and patient are caught, the problem worsens and to resolve it become central to the therapy. There is no borderline where Hermes can move, where he can dance with the nymph and even deal with her mania, knowing that, in spite of it, psyche can move, enabling the analytical relationship to go on.

Throughout our discussion of the classical image of Hermes chasing a nymph, we have been moving our awareness of the image to the point where it touches upon rape, maintaining the borderline between chasing and rape. I consider rape to be within that borderline where it is either a psychic mover or what is considered collectively as being within the context of crime. Whatever the motif of rape means for the psyche has not as yet been worked out in psychology because, like so many other images, it cannot be defined or conceptualized and, even less, symbolized.

The final and third variation on our theme of Hermes chasing a nymph is that of trying to explore some of the facets which may be components of the Hermes style of rape.

Greek and Roman mythology offer a catalogue of rapes still waiting to be studied psychologically: centaurs raping women; centaurs and heroes raping Amazons; Zeus as a bull raping Europa; Poseidon as a stallion raping Demeter, in the form of a mare; rapes of boys and rapes of girls; and, of course, the rape of Persephone. The rape of the Sabines offers a variation of the motif by linking it specifically with the mythology of the foundation of a city, in this case, Rome.

Mediterranean classical mythology is crowded with rapes. We do not know the exact occurrence of rape in ancient classical culture, although we do know the approximate extent of its iconography as the main motif linking the Middle Ages and the Renaissance with the ancient world. Jean Seznec writes: "If one attempts to recall, for example, the profane themes most often treated in Italy at this time [15th and 16th century], what comes first to mind are the scenes of seduction or rape, of love or drunken revelry..."[18] We cannot enumerate or make a list of the motif of rape since the Renaissance because its imagery is as overwhelming as it has always been. Just to take Picasso's imagery of rape and to try to differentiate and enumerate the number of rapes in his art would be an enormous task.

When we read in the daily news the statistics of rape, our feeling of alarm is caused by the amount, and we tend to forget that this same quantity has always been present in Western culture. In any case, the imagery of rape today does not differ so very much from its imagery as handed down by classic writers, poets, and painters, though it does not have

18. Seznec, *The Survival of the Pagan Gods, op. cit.,* p. 5; also footnote 6, in which he gives the references for the lists that have been compiled of the images on this theme.

the grace they achieved with this motif. We have no record of how rape was reported in ancient times, or we have to accept the reportage in terms of the quantity of rapes recorded in the imagery of the classical myths. For example, if we take the *Iliad* as the cultural source of Western man, the most immediate action at the beginning has to do with the rape of Bryseida and Chryseida. We also know that the enormous effort of mobilizing the Greek expeditionary force to Troy had at its origin another rape: the seduction and rape of Helen by Paris. I think this tells us more about the importance of rape in human nature than any numerical statistics.

Today, rape is generally viewed as a criminal offense and is the concern of legal psychiatry, though the judges who deal with these cases do have some difficulty in evaluating what is considered to be legally criminal. Rape still catches the imagination of writers, painters, and filmmakers and is one of the main motifs of the era. During the early naive days of Hollywood, the rapist appeared with a top hat, a moustache, and, to the children of those days, with rather sinister, weird eyes. He was an image of 'fear' and 'horror' that remained in the memory, but which, with the passage of time, came to have a tremendously comic touch. Western films offer an inexhaustible amount of rape that is easier to connect mythologically: there are centaurs, heroes, Amazons, virgins, and so on; the motif of rape appears again and again. In whichever way it occurs, in films, novels, paintings, in fantasies and dreams brought into psychotherapy, in whatever context, the motif of rape always has an impact of horror, of pathology, sometimes of a crime. In psychotherapy, however, its impact activates very deep complexes that are of great therapeutical value, as we shall see later.

Kraft-Ebbing, in 1880, coined the psychiatric term 'sadomasochism,' a term based on the works of Marquis de Sade and Leopold Sacher-Masoch. The works of these two men introduced a coinage into our language that has been totally accepted by this epoch; even a lady over a cup of tea has an awareness of this terminology and uses it with certain

insights. And within the personal variations of each psychiatrist and psychotherapist, there is also an awareness of, and
insight into, this concept in the field of psychology. I have
not come across any direct reference to either de Sade's or
Sacher-Masoch's literature in the works of Freud and Jung;
undoubtedly their insights came not through its actual
imagery, but via its conceptualization in Kraft-Ebbing. I have
made this little detour so that we bear in mind that sado-
masochism has tended to be seen as a concept or a diagnosis
of a condition, but its images, from which we can reflect the
perversity of a history, have not been explored sufficiently. I
would like to see the images of sado-masochism as having
archetypal roots in humankind, and as offering a spectrum
that can be viewed in psychotherapy as the demand of a part
of nature in need of being lived. There is no doubt that
Kraft-Ebbing's coinage has had a powerful impact on modern psychology, as well as on modern medicine.

If the influence of this concept has been so profound on
daily life, psychology, and medicine, Mario Praz, in his
Romantic Agony[19] skillfully reveals the equally profound
influence the works of the Marquis de Sade have had on
nineteenth-century literature, which can be seen as an
antecedent of today's overwhelming images of horror
shown in newspapers, television, and films. Praz tracks down
the appearance of horror in Western literature within a
historical perspective, calling our attention to, and challenging us, to study its psychological implications. It seems to be
horror for horror's sake, something we see in the public's
predilection for horror films today.

We have just referred to sado-masochism and the profusion of horror imagery. Both stem from the historically most
repressed gods with their archetypal forms (above all,
Dionysus with his sense of tragedy) and the rituals and
imagery of death. Accepting this premise, I suggest that
sado-masochism and horror imagery can be added to the

---

19. Mario Praz, *The Romantic Agony,* trans. Angus Davidson (Oxford
University Press Paperback, 1970).

historical appearances of the imagery of rape, but have now been given a bizarre expression, without any of the grace given to it by the classic poet-mythographers or the nineteenth-century novelists. Perhaps now, in all this pile of horror, we can begin to see the expression of a basic need,[20] probably pointing to the primitive man's level of adolescent initiation through horror, the perennial need of the man (that old horror-room of initiation in us all). "... the backward half-look / Over the shoulder, towards the primitive terror."[21] Seen within its historical perspective, we can be connected backwards to rape in classical times and even further back to that primordial image of rape and horror, with its connection to the most primitive and instinctual level of the psyche. Yes, the image of Hermes chasing a nymph, described so beautifully by the classic poets, contains within itself that event in the deepest and most obscure times of primitive man when the first man raped the first nymph.

The repercussion of horror in the soul is the concern of psychotherapy. The first time the therapist is presented with an image of horror, it can be so horrifying that he reacts by trying to repress it, either by putting it down with a psychiatric coinage or by reducing it to the patient's causalistic and personal history. An image of horror in dreams can be especially upsetting for a therapist without the background or attitude for dealing with it, believing with the faith of all believers that the patient is in a bad mental condition because of the horror images brought with him into psychotherapy; that the therapist's office is to cure the patient's illness by getting rid of the images of horror. There is no awareness that these very images arise, firstly, to compensate the patient's nature and, secondly, to be recognized as an

20. It is interesting to note the age of many of the writers of Romantic horror literature. Mary Shelley, for instance, was only nineteen when she wrote *Frankenstein*, which induces us to view fantasies of horror as an element of adolescent initiation. Youth would seem to be the time when, archetypally, the imagery of horror needs to appear.
21. Eliot, *Four Quartets, op. cit.*, "The Dry Salvages."

expression of the need for initiation through horror. Furthermore, I would suggest our aim should be to detect the horror image in the complex, not for diagnostic purposes, but to provide a view more suited to the patient's nature. If, basically speaking, psychotherapy is to compensate, then we have to stick to the images of horror, for, even though we can neither understand them nor make much sense of them, it is these images which can compensate. All we can do is to withstand these images of horror, even when they appear profusely, until nature begins to metamorphose them into a more understandable psychic expression; for example, into a more commodious depression or individual view of life.

Medieval man gave more value to images of horror, as Miss Frances Yates' marvelous scholarship transmits:

> And now the *imagines agentes* make their appearance, quoted in full from Tullius. Remarkably beautiful or hideous, dressed in crown and purple garments, deformed or disfigured with blood or mud, smeared with red paint, comic or ridiculous, they stroll mysteriously, like players, out of antiquity into the scholastic treatise on memory as part of Prudence. The solution emphasizes that the reason for the choice of such images is that they 'move strongly' and so adhere to the soul.[22]

This evaluation of horror images offers a suggestion for psychotherapy, namely to conceive of them in terms of psychic-movers, contained in the memory (the main instrument of psychotherapy), and part of what is probably the psychotherapeutic virtue *par excellence* – Prudence. With the help of Prudence we can evaluate more accurately the image of horror in relation to the personality of the patient. It is Prudence that moves us into the art of dosage: dosing the image carefully and then leaving it to be assimilated.

When I first wrote about rape and horror I confess I had more intuition than experience; now I feel my intuition and experience are more balanced, the experience of years

---

22. Yates, *The Art of Memory, op. cit.,* pp. 66-67.

supporting that earlier intuition, enabling it to see better and even take some risks. I do not want here to describe my experiences with images of rape and horror; suffice it to say that by experience I mean roughly: being more acquainted with the imagery of horror. I have gained a certain prudence which allows me to withstand a long series of horror images, and, above all, a deeper and more subjective evaluation of their compensatory function in the psyche. I simply want to suggest that a hermetic psychotherapy has neither aim, goal, purposefulness nor meaning, all of which can bring a life to a standstill; the only concern of Hermes as lord of the roads is to move along the new roads of the psyche, and that the psyche moves.

Surely the time is constellated for rape and horror to be included in the studies of psychology. There are two contributions in this respect: Niel Micklem in his paper "On Hysteria"[23] takes one specific rape – the rape of Persephone by Hades, in the form of Pluto – and works it out as being the 'cure' for hysteria. Micklem presents an archetypal picture of hysteria, centered on the mythologem of the mother, Demeter, suffocating her daughter, Persephone. The scene comes in the early part of the Homeric "Hymn to Demeter" and it is upon this myth that the Eleusinian mysteries were based. This archetypal suffocation of the daughter by the mother is the imagery at the root of the hysterical condition, the cause of hysteria.

Micklem discusses whether or not hysteria is an illness: if it is an illness, then, like any other illness, it is its quantitative aspect that gives the diagnosis. In any event, it has an archetypal root and, therefore, is part of human nature, in both men and women; and it manifests itself here and there, mostly unnoticed, in our daily lives. Micklem's doubts over this issue imply that it is both an illness and not an illness, depending upon its many guises, its autonomy in the person, and to what extent it pervades our daily life. For

23. Niel Micklem, "On Hysteria: The Mythical Syndrome," *Spring 1974* (Spring Publications: Zurich, 1974), p. 147ff.

Micklem, the 'cure' for this condition is what happens in the mythologem in opposition to the mother's suffocation of the daughter, namely, the rape of Persephone by Hades/ Pluto. This 'cure' can be equated with the person moving out of the hysterical, two-dimensional, repetitive, paralyzing suffocation into an awakening of the repressed psychic body (the rape by Pluto into the underworld), out of which new images emerge to participate in life and enrich the personality. It is a specific psychic rape, and when it happens, usually through dreams and accompanied by images of horror and pain, we have to remember that it is Pluto, the personification of death itself, creating tragic emotional horror. But, at the same time, according to Micklem and my own experience, it is what produces the 'cure' that has to be seen as a psychic movement away from the exhausting repetition of hysterical suffocation into a deeper and more consistent awareness of the personality.

Needless to say, it is pointless to go into explanatory rationalizations of this kind of imagery with the patient. The patient's projections upon an image of rape and death still come from the hysterical pole that has been ruling life. It needs time for the image to begin to move the patient's psyche in the opposite direction, towards a more corporeal realm of the psyche.

The second contribution, Alfred Ziegler's *Archetypal Medicine*,[24] considers the image of horror at the psychosomatic level of nature. It is a thought-provoking book, particularly in relation to what we are concerned with here. In his therapeutical ideas, death and horror are center-stage. He takes the Jungian conception of the compensatory opposites and carries it into the psychosomatic realm, where physical illness can be seen as a compensation, being diagnosed through the images of horror the illness expresses. He looks into man's psychosomatic nature, which he imagines as man's chimerical nature, where man's illnesses are 'programmed' and 'designed.'[25] This idea suggests that our

24. Alfred Ziegler, *Archetypal Medicine*, "Theoria," *op. cit.*

psychosomatic balance depends upon the strange connection we can make to our chimerical nature and its horror. Moreover, through the chimera, Ziegler entices us to reevaluate a whole range of images of horror clustered around it, and this in turn moves into a reevaluation of the appearance of images of horror in dreams that, traditionally, has been taken as negative. In my own case, he has added to my study of the archetypes, which was based mostly on Homer's legacy of consistent archetypal images, stimulating me to go into Hesiod and to become more aware of images which have not been of much concern to the studies of the archetypes. But I consider it to be an imagery which can lead us to have a more accurate lense for focusing on the intimate biological level of man's nature, an imagery more suited to a psychosomatically oriented psychotherapy, or to a psychotherapy which does not leave out the psychosomatic expression of nature. Following Ziegler, I am proposing a new adventure with Hermes into a psychic realm as yet unexplored, a realm where Hermes is the only possible guide, though we have to remember that he can also lead us astray.

The most immediate reaction to Ziegler's conception of the psychosomatic is that either one connects to the horror one carries at the innermost level of one's nature or one can become an actual image of horror through an illness. Furthermore, if this is valid for psychosomatic medicine, then it is also valid for psychopathology, since it is accepted that in psychotic and schizophrenic patients images associated with the chimera are to the fore, often the Medusa, as Micklem has worked out.[26] Ziegler centers his therapy of some morbidities in the reflection on and connection to death, and has chosen the traditional medieval image of the

25. Ziegler's idea has the particularity of denoting the shadow of the Calvinistic doctrine of predestination: nature predestines our illnesses. For me, this has further implications, since it brings tragedy into the case history; the tragic higher consciousness implies predestination.

26. Niel Micklem, "The Intolerable Image," *Spring 1979* (Spring Publications: Zurich, 1979).

Todeshochzeit, the wedding with death, for this purpose. I would add that the image of marriage with death is valid for the therapy of any sort of illness. How to deal with and reflect the constellation of the *Todeshochzeit,* especially in dreams, requires, however, all the therapist's art, as does the imagery of rape, which is implicitly a wedding with death.

Let us take up again the seemingly innocent, bucolic image of Hermes chasing a nymph, in which, so far, we have seen cheap sexuality and love by chance. It is an erotica that I would like the reader to imagine as resulting in rape, a fortuitous rape, and to include this image within the wider constellation of Hermes in psychotherapy. It is possible then to imagine this fortuitous rape as another epiphany of Hermes, one in which hermetic rape happens, in which both the therapist's and the patient's nymphs are raped by the therapeutical Hermes, who is in the middle of the relationship. I would not like any misunderstanding in this respect: it would be a fatal mistake to conceive the therapist as rapist, for that would be to deny that this image is archetypal, as well as what it has to offer as a psychic mover.

A constellation of rape in psychotherapy is propitious for dealing with images of horror and death that, sometimes, are one and the same. Let me put it plainly: if a discussion moves into the imagery of death, I would call this, in itself, a rape.[27] It requires a hermetic consciousness that gives to the therapist the indirection and art for reflecting this kind of imagery in such a way that there is a chance it might adhere to the patient's soul. In a wider context, we can also say, there is always a nymph in us that can be raped by Hermes, rape as dynamism, as a basic psychic need, that, again and again, violates our psyche. The rape contained in the image of Hermes chasing a nymph is a happening that can come about at any given moment, and so has nothing whatsoever

27. It is through the reflection of Hermes as rapist that I insight Dr. H.K. Fierz's misunderstood conception of a neurosis or psychosis being cured in a few minutes. I see this kind of possible quick cure as a meeting of Hermes raping a nymph and the synchronistic time of therapist and patient.

to do with a premeditated conception of psychotherapy. I believe by now that it will not be too difficult for the reader to accept the complexities of this image – its relaxed bucolic scenery, the love by chance, the rape, the images of horror and death – and its validity for both men and women.

*
* *

Among students of psychology there is a figure more popular than the Marquis de Sade: Don Juan, who can be seen, metaphorically, as a bridge linking the classical image of rape to the "Divine Marquis" and his followers. He forms a bridge connecting us to the Mediterranean classical roots of rape and to that same archetype of rape as it moved, under a new distortion, into the 'romantic agony.' There is an enormous amount of literature about Don Juan. Apart from the oral tradition, he appears in the writings of Tirso de Molina, Zamora, de Bury, Molière, Byron, Dumas, Merimée, Zorrilla, etc. Don Juan, from his first appearance in the Golden Age of Spanish literature, has a sufficient pedigree to be considered as yet another rapist in the old Mediterranean tradition. The Spanish Don Juan is a figure that connects to the essential, constant image of rape, to rape as imagined by the Marquis de Sade, and to the psychopathic rape of today. For the last variation on our theme I shall attempt to connect Don Juan with the image of Hermes chasing a nymph, and for this purpose I shall limit myself to Zorrilla's play *Don Juan Tenorio*.[28]

There are two ingredients in the Spanish Don Juan which I would like to just touch upon in order to help us focus on our main interest: Don Juan as rapist. The first is the Iberio-Celtic folklore motif of challenging death (kicking the skull),[29] an obvious symbol of evil, which means a psychopathic contempt for death. It is important to pay attention to this contempt, because in the psychopathic personality,

28. José Zorrilla, *Don Juan Tenorio* (Taurus: Madrid, 1967).

whose characteristic, as I have worked out,[30] is to have no images, the image of all images – death, is missing. The second is the 'estatuas parlantes,' the animation of the statue.[31] In psychotherapy, when a statue appears in a dream it is an indication of what is dead or petrified in us, marking what is in need of movement.[32] In the case of Don Juan, what is petrified (the statue of Don Gonzalo) challenges him to a situation in which he cannot give his usual response; he cannot kill what he has already killed.

Besides rape, the connection between the Spanish Don Juan and the French libertine is the enumeration. In Zorrilla's play there is an enumeration of rape and murder between Don Juan and Don Luis. In the Marquis de Sade's work the enumeration includes these elements but with more oddities, being more concerned with the number of debaucheries. This numbering of rapes, murders, and debaucheries, the latter described in terms of an extraordinary precision (colors, odors, lashes, time, etc.), and measurement (usually size of sexual organs), is a psychology expressed within its own *raison d'être,* and is undoubtedly connected to the mythology of rape. If enumeration makes

29. A motif thoroughly worked out by Victor Said Armesto in his *La Leyenda de Don Juan* (Espasa-Calpe: Buenos Aires, 1946), and also touched upon by Marie-Louise von Franz in *Shadow and Evil in Fairy Tales* (Spring Publications: Zurich and New York, 1974).

30. Rafael Lopez-Pedraza, "Moon Madness - Titanic Love: A Meeting of Pathology and Poetry" in *Images of the Untouched* (Pegasus: Dallas, 1982); and "On Cultural Anxiety" in *Symbolic and Clinical Approaches in Practice and Theory, op. cit.*

31. For the importance of this element during the Renaissance, see Frances Yates, *Giordano Bruno and the Hermetic Tradition, op. cit.,* where she includes the sources of the animation of the statue in the Hellenistic *Corpus Hermeticum* in which the fantasies go back to the Egyptians. In *Don Juan Tenorio* the motif appears within a variation.

32. The first dream a student of literature had during his psychotherapy was of the stone-carved tomb of a great poet. On the top of this tomb was the allegorical motif of a swan, also carved in stone. Discussion of the dream gave evidence that something was petrified in his literary studies; his logos = swan (Apollo) was also petrified and needed to be 'animated.'

us think in terms of initiation – in this case, the initiation into the realm of rape and horror – there is also the psychopathic side that resists initiation. I cannot think of initiation when there is a psychopathic lacuna and the endless repetition of petrified schemes learned mimetically, for they tell us of a life in which psyche does not exist: the so-called soul-less personality. We have to differentiate between the soul-making aspect of the fantasy of rape, where initiation and healing can happen, and the psychopathic side, where neither initiation, healing, nor psychic movement can happen, before we consider a hermetic borderline where these two elements in human nature can meet.

The difference between the therapeutical initiatory side and sheer psychopathy is that, in the soul-making process, there are images and no enumeration, whereas enumeration predominates in the psychopathic side. When the images of a man's love-affairs come into his mind, connecting him to the many complexes of his history, it is very different from those love-affairs coming into his mind in terms of number: "I have had twenty love-affairs." It is the number of murders and rapes that draw our attention in Zorrilla's *Don Juan Tenorio.* Don Juan memorizes his history in terms of quantitative enumeration, never in images, as far as I know. Images are not possible for him. It is the precision in the enumeration of debaucheries which the Marquis de Sade has transmitted to us, mainly in his encyclopedic record of *120 Days of Sodom.*[33] This enumeration is fundamental to the psychology of both Don Juan and de Sade.

Pierre Jean Jouve comments on its importance in his discussion of Mozart's *Don Juan:*

> Noteworthy is the important part played by the enumeration of countries and numbers, symbol of erotic compulsion – enumeration replaces physical possession. The whole Catalogue

---

33. Marquis de Sade, *One Hundred and Twenty Days of Sodom and Other Writings,* Austryn and Seaver, Richard eds. (Grove Press: New York, 1966).

Aria is constructed to lead up to an expansion of the glorious phrase: Mà in Ispagna – son già mille e trè – "But in Spain there are already one thousand and three..."[34]

So numbers and counting seem to be how what we call psychopathy, or the psychopathic personality, memorizes. Through this enumeration there is probably an 'ordering' in the personality which marks the frame of reference of this kind of behavior that is able to count destruction with precision. We can see something of this aspect of the psychology of psychopathy in the tradition of naval punishment (the number of lashes) and in the delinquent's knowledge of the exact punishment he will receive for whatever misdeed. Also it is worth noting how today's periodicals enumerate the exact number of deaths and casualties that occur around the world.

Don Juan, in belonging to the classical Mediterranean tradition of the rapists, is an archetypal link to the sadistic bizarreness of the 'Divine Marquis.'[35] I want to establish that not only sexuality and rape, but also debauchery and psychopathy have a connection to the image of Hermes chasing a nymph. In this chasing of the nymph, we shall never know – in psychotherapy, in life, or in reading the literature about Don Juan and of the Marquis de Sade and his followers – if the archetype is going to fall into a soul-making process, psychopathy, or even into criminality. Let me repeat once again that implicit in the fantasy of rape is that borderline in which either soul-making or delinquency can occur.

All I have discussed so far about rape might seem to be a long detour, but it is part of my intention of presenting Don Juan as a link to the classical imagery of rape. If we reflect upon the way in which the motif of rape has flooded Western culture, the literary and psychological bibliography

34. Pierre Jean Jouve, *Mozart's Don Juan,* trans. Eric Earnshaw Smith (Vincent Stuart: London, 1957), p. 29.
35. Saint-Paulien, *Don Juan: Mito y Realidad,* Edisven, S.A., 1969.

of the Don Juan motif alone numbers over five thousand items.

In Zorrilla's *Don Juan Tenorio,* it is easy to see that no sexual fantasies or images appear: the action goes straight into seduction, rape, and murder. Don Juan and Don Luis discuss the number of their rapes and crimes, very well presented in two separate lists for the sake of clarity ("mayor claridad").

> *Don Luis*
> You are right indeed
> Here is mine; look,
> separated by a line
> I bring the names properly written
> to make them clearer.

> *Don Juan*
> Arranged in the same way
> I bring my accounts
> in two separate lines
> the dead by challenge
> and the women seduced.
> Count.

> *Don Luis*
> Count.

> *Don Juan*
> Twenty-three.

> *Don Luis*
> Those are the dead. Let me see yours.
> By the cross of Saint Andrew!
> Here the adding is thirty-two.

> *Don Juan*
> Those are the dead.

> *Don Luis*
> That is to kill.

> *Don Juan*
> I exceed you by nine.

> *Don Luis*
> You defeat me.
> Let us go on to the conquests.

> *Don Juan*
> I count here fifty-six.

> *Don Luis*
> And I count in your list
> seventy-two.

> *Don Juan*
> So you lose.[36]

Don Juan counts Don Luis' dead as numbering twenty-three, and Don Luis counts Don Juan's numbering thirty-two. Of rapes ("conquistas"), Don Juan counts fifty-six in Don Luis' list and Don Luis counts seventy-two in Don Juan's list. After all this enumeration, Don Luis points out the only element missing in Don Juan's list.

> *Don Luis*
> Fairly, you have but one lack.

> *Don Juan*
> Could you point it out to me?

> *Don Luis*
> Yes indeed; a novice
> about to profess.[37]

---

36. Zorrilla, *Don Juan Tenorio, op. cit.*, pp. 211-212 (My translation).
37. *Ibid.*, p. 212.

This is the challenge which brings about the climax of the play: the ultimate challenge of the most extreme fantasy of rape possible: to rape a novice nun, a virgin girl who is preparing to be a bride of Christ, the God that died on the cross. We must not forget that *Don Juan Tenorio* belongs to the imagery of the Spanish religious tradition: Tirso de Molina, the first who wrote about Don Juan, became a priest, and the play was written to be performed on All Souls Day. The challenge of Don Luis to Don Juan to rape a novice about to profess should be read in this context, but, at the same time, it links to the image of Hermes chasing a nymph.

Now it would have been risky to make this link to Hermes chasing a nymph had it not been for a short classical line which is as valid as a long story: "The first Cupid is said to be the son of Mercury and the first Diana..."[38] Cicero tells us of a love-affair between Mercury (Hermes, our rapist) and Diana (Artemis, principle of religious virginity). But Cicero's line also moves our imagination to that primordial image of the first man who chased and raped a nymph, as if, in using the word 'first,' Cicero was touching the archetypal core of the image of Hermes chasing a nymph. In this sense, the image reaches down to a deep and primal level of the psyche; and in spite of the bucolic grace depicted by the classic poet-mythographers, the image has a level of primordial horror and fills us with pain and fear, affecting our emotional body and leaving us paralyzed and perplexed.

As we have seen, psychotherapy in depth cannot leave out the imagery of horror and its emotions. It is essential as it connects to death, the opposite of hysteria, as worked out by Micklem, and as Ziegler understands it with his psychosomatic conception. For me, as a therapist whose main concern is the psyche, no matter what the condition of the patient, the bucolic graceful image of Hermes chasing a

38. Cicero, *De Natura Deorum*, III, xxiii, 60 (Loeb Library, Heinemann: London), pp. 343-345.

nymph and the imagery it provokes is a particularly suitable vehicle, within the confines of psychotherapy, for reaching this emotional level of the psyche. I feel this sort of image is most akin to my tradition and personal complexities, just as Ziegler's expressionist *Todeshochzeit* is the product of his culture and race.

In this third tale, Cicero furthers the imagery of Hermes chasing a nymph by introducing Artemis herself, the goddess of virginity in nature. Instead of a nymph such as Polymele, or the tale of a nymph within a tale, such as told by the goddess of love, Aphrodite, in one simple line, like an old fragment or a modern telegram, Cicero tells the whole story within a thoroughly archetypal configuration – two gods and a goddess. Here, there are no inconsistent nymphs or mortals; the line is archetypal and gives us a strong basis from which to insight the complexities I have been working out. On the other hand, in the way in which Don Luis challenges Don Juan, we approach the tension in the erotic fantasy that is the ultimate challenge: to rape a novice nun. However, the chase results not in Eros but in dishonor, murder, and death. Cicero's image and the image in *Don Juan Tenorio* give us an insight into that borderline between the totally archetypal fantasy of Hermes with Artemis resulting in Eros, and the disaster of the challenge in Don Juan. For we have the impression there are indeed archetypal images behind his destructive deeds, his pleasure in doing wrong, and that this wrong-doing, including concrete rape and killing, could be seen as having a connection to the mythologem of Artemis with its religious connotations.

There is something pathetic in the way Don Juan tries in vain to connect to his soul. Further on in the play he seems to have a certain awareness of his damnation, and it is not until there is no other possibility that at last he has the vague fantasy of finding salvation. He dies within the impossibility of this attempt. This final scene of the play depicts a constancy in the psychology of the psychopath: a longing for salvation that is far beyond the reach of his nature. I sometimes wonder if the notion of salvation as spiritual, religious salvation has a psychopathic background, an attainment never to be realized, or only to be 'achieved' through the illusion of psychopathic mimetism. At the same time, Don Juan's longing for salvation can be seen as a tragic image evoking pity, the pity we feel for the psychopath outside and inside ourselves. *Don Juan Tenorio* is about the challenge of the forbidden image of the Virgin, but also presents us with a picture, perhaps one of the best, of what psychiatry in the late nineteenth century coined as psychopathic behavior.

In this chapter, I have been trying to track down the archetypal connections behind rape, from its imagery as a psychic-mover to crime. We have found in psychopathic behavior that the quantitative side is important, both the extent and the enumeration. We have discussed numbers as being connected with sexual oddities and psychopathy, and we have attempted to view these things from an archetypal background. Classic Jungian psychology has worked out the extraordinary connection of numbers with the ordering principle of the self. Let us take for example, the axiom of Maria Prophetissa with which Jung begins his interpretation of the tenth image of the "Rosarium Philosophorum":

> Our last picture is the tenth of the series, and this is certainly no accident, for the denarius is supposed to be the perfect number. We have shown that the axiom of Maria consists of 4,3,2,1; the sum of these numbers is 10, which stands for unity on a higher level.[39]

The insight into numbers as symbols (symbolism, function of symbolization) belongs to old traditions.[40] There are many numbers, as is the case with the axiom of Maria, which, when they appear in the psyche, order and balance the personality. I would like to suggest that these numbers create this order because, behind their symbolization, the

39. C.G. Jung, *CW* 16, para. 525; also footnote 1, where he gives a detailed explanation of the number 10.
40. C.G. Jung, *Psychological Types, op. cit.,* p. 601.

psyche is connecting to the most disturbing aspect of the unconscious, to what we have been calling psychopathy or, to use a more religious word, to the evil we tend to exclude from our 'process of individuation.' Though I leave further speculation to my reader, it is easy to conceive, for instance, that numbers and counting can exclude those images of horror, those psychic movers, by replacing their unbearable impact. For the sake of continuing this line of thought, one cannot avoid being struck, when reading either *Don Juan Tenorio* or the works of de Sade, by the strange exaltation of the personality induced by this counting. It is perhaps an expression of a peculiar kind of a 'wholeness.'

In conceiving number symbolism in this way – as a function of balance in the psyche – we are open to the possibility that throughout culture, number symbolism and its systems – Pythagorean, religious, alchemical, Cabbalistic, etc. – could be ways of dealing with the psychotic realm of the psyche. Therefore, and this is well within the context of Jungian thought, it is not so farfetched for psychotherapy to conceive numbers, counting, measurement, chronological time, as connecting us with what we call psychopathic. Behind the container of symbolic numbers is that part of the psyche where those elements lurk which would otherwise be expressed in perversions, sado-masochism, sexual oddities, religious and political psychopathic behavior, or even ill-ness. Behind the container of number symbolism are images of horror, those images which most move the psyche. I hope that my contention of the borderline between the emotional soul-image and psychopathy is beginning to become clearer through this distinction between numbers and images. I hope it will help us towards a new level of differentiation of what is one of the main intentions of this book: to differentiate between symbols and images, two words so often interchangeable in psycho-logical writing. As we have seen, however, they are different in what they represent in psychotherapy.

Implicit in our discussion of rape and horror in relation to the mythological image of Hermes chasing a nymph and the damnation of Don Juan is an attempt to attain some differentiation in a great bulk of material which is usually lumped together in terms of shadow. The image of horror has tended to be seen in terms of shadow, the technical Jungian term to refer to what we are not aware of in our own nature, but which we have to become aware of; in relation to Don Juan and the psychopath, this would be the evil we have to reject. Neither Don Juan nor the psychopath have been viewed as images of horror in themselves, images which hit with their own searing emotion, perturb and thus compensate, "'move strongly' and so adhere to the soul."[41]

41. Frances Yates, *The Art of Memory, op. cit.,* p. 67.

Chapter VI

Priapus

There was another God "numbered among the sons of Hermes."[1] His name was Priapus. "... It was publicly said of him that he was both father and son to Hermes,"[2] therefore he filled both roles. Also "... it was claimed for him that he was none other than the Hermaphroditus."[3] With Aphrodite as his mother, he was said to have various other fathers: "Dionysus, or sometimes Adonis, or even Zeus himself."[4] In introducing this god, let us take together, simultaneously, all the components I have just mentioned – father and son, the claim of being Hermaphroditus, plus the validity of his three other fathers, Dionysus, Adonis, and Zeus. For a study of the complexities of this god, it seems to me the only way.

I am aware that this intention could be upsetting from a scholarly point of view, but I am reflecting from the angle of psychotherapy.

It seems to me that these fragments of rather obscure classical tales gather together elements from which we can have a first picture of the psychology of Priapus. Karl Kerényi assembled these fragments in his book, *The Gods of the Greeks*, where, if we are lucky, we can read on just one or two pages enough to form an image. But we must appreciate that those pages were written after Kerényi had worked on a

1. Kerényi, *The Gods of the Greeks, op. cit.*, p. 176.
2. *Ibid.*, p. 175.
3. *Ibid.*, p. 176.
4. *Ibid.*, p. 176.

large bulk of classical literature.[5] I am also aware that even the most audacious psychologist might be upset by such an extreme lack of differentiation, calling it a *mixtum compositum*. But it is precisely within this peculiar *mixtum* (mixing of archetypes?) that we are able to have a closer psychological view of the image of Priapus. The challenge for our imagination is to at least try to read the image within the complexities of all these components. For it is our imagination that reads the image. We need to learn how to read images.

The image of Priapus being both a father and a son is certainly a very confusing one. And it becomes even more confusing when the father, who can also be the son, is Hermes, whose characteristic line is not exactly that of a father. In any event, the father-son relationship is extraordinarily confused. The image conveys the atmosphere of a very peculiar family situation, marking with this peculiarity a relationship of its own to life. It is a confusion that also probably marks a different relationship and erotica among men than the ones I discussed in the chapter on Dryops. Moreover, this confusion in the father-son relationship is stressed if we accept the three other fathers – Dionysus, Adonis, and Zeus – with all the complexes they add to the image of Priapus.

The story of Priapus' birth was one more in the series modelled on mis-begettings: "... Aphrodite had borne a child so monstrous – with a huge tongue and a mighty belly, a creature excessively phallic, and indeed phallic to the rear..."[6] This image of Priapus, transmitted to us from classical times, is of a grotesque scarecrow. His place, probably more in Hellenistic and Roman times than in that of classical Greece, was the garden, the place where, supposedly, the erotica of Priapus was enacted. Nowadays, since gardens are no longer so important, his erotica appears in

5. For those interested: G. *Kaibel, Epigrammata Graeca ex lapidus collecta, Hygini fabulae, Lucianus, Jupiter Tragoedus, Lycophron, Nonnus commentator Gregorii Nazianzeni, Apollonius Rhodius*, etc.
6. Kerényi, *The Gods of the Greeks, op. cit.*, p. 176.

parks, cinemas, on staircases, in bars, in special places where a look gains admission, and in little exhibitionist acts here and there.

The conception of Priapus as a fertility god of plants and animals is not relevant to this book. By generalizing this god in terms of fertility, the image vanishes. It is the same as saying that the ass, the animal sacrificed in the Priapus cult, is an animal of fertility. We know the ass has a connection to Dionysus, one of the fathers of Priapus, and here there is perhaps an element of animal fertility, but we also know, following this same Dionysian complex, that the ass, with its phallic element, has other connections more suited to the study of psychology. The ass, in its phallic appearance, has a better connection to Priapus, enabling us to view it within its tradition of the comedian, the fool, the stupid, and the obscene[7] – aspects of Priapus which are indeed relevant elements to familiarize ourselves with, since they are central to the image of the patient whose personality is ruled by Priapus.

Now, if we keep this image of Priapus, this obscene, grotesque scarecrow of a god, and bear in mind the immense complexity within his image, we can get at what today has become an awareness, and a very psychological one, since there is a god, Priapus, son (or father) of Hermes behind it. It is today's awareness of the freak. The appearance of the freak in our times is perhaps more important than we realize. Today's use of the word 'freak,' a word that has appeared among the youth of the new life-style, contains an awareness of the image of Priapus and his archetypal manifestation in the body and behavior. We talk about someone as being a 'freak,' 'freakish,' or 'freaking out.' With these words we are expressing an awareness of the realm of this archetype. Nowadays, the vision of the other in this respect is more in the open, less ambiguous than that

7. Cf. William Willeford, *The Fool and His Sceptre* (Northwestern Univ. Press, 1969), for the connection between the ass, the fool, and the comedian.

English camouflage of saying that so-and-so has become 'rather peculiar' or eccentric. Because it is manifesting itself so openly, the freak is easier to detect than it was some years ago and, of course, easier to detect in ourselves. When an archetype makes its appearance on the stage of life and history, it can move either center-stage or backstage, as the case may be. The new historical manifestation of this archetype is obvious. Daily, we see men and women in the streets claiming, with the image they offer, to be Hermaphroditus.

There have been many great artists, with a keen eye for detecting the freak, who have left us a rich legacy in this respect. I would like to mention just a few: Velasquez, Goya, Ribera, Toulouse-Lautrec, and Picasso. They have given us a reflection of body freakishness which, because it is archetypal, speaks to us all. Velasquez's paintings on this theme [Plate 9] are testimony to an awareness coming from his association with the atmosphere of the royal court during a time when freakishness was closer to the 'consciousness' of the ruling principle. Robert Massie describes royalty's attraction to freakishness during the seventeenth and eighteenth centuries: Frederick William I of Prussia was obsessed with his collection of giants, for which he was renowned throughout Europe. The best way to find favor with the King of Prussia was to send him a giant to put into one of the two battalions of giants he kept, with which he played like a child, as if they were enormous living toys. Peter the Great's attraction was to dwarfs: to amuse himself and the aristocracy, he arranged and attended the marriage of two dwarfs; later, at the celebration of the birth of his son (the second Peter), a well-shaped woman dwarf stepped out of a pie, stark naked except for a headdress and some ornaments of red ribbons, made a speech and drank several healths with wine she had with her in the pie. At his wife's table, a man dwarf was served up in a similar manner.[8] A faint echo of this atmosphere was expressed in a photograph of the

8. Robert K. Massie, *Peter the Great* (Ballantine: New York, 1986), pp. 597 and 688.

Plate 9

funeral of Salazar, the Portuguese dictator. Mounting guard at the foot of his coffin stood a giant and a dwarf.

Ribera's painting shocks our eyes and our sense of body reality with the unexpectedly freakish Hermaphroditic imagery in a portrayal of two Castilian peasants [Plate 10].

Goya lived during the turmoil that was Spain at the turn of the eighteenth-century, but he also lived a turmoil in his own soul. He was a genius, a forerunner of nineteenth-century art. His paintings, with their exploration of the darkest inner imagery of man, express a uniquely strong psychology that will always speak to our sensibility. In his marvelous drawing, "Loco Picaro," his view of the freak gives an impression of a confused pathology of madness and the picaresque, expressed in the hermaphroditism of a peculiar pregnancy [Plate 11].

The sensibility of Toulouse-Lautrec, a very strange man who suffered the freak in his body, has left us a heritage of art and humanness in which the circus, the freak, and the prostitute are the main subjects. His work is the testimony of an epoch – the Belle Époque. We can see how he viewed another artist – Oscar Wilde [Plate 12].

The Gothic period, for some historians the peak of Western culture, seems to have had a profound awareness of the freak, the monstrous side of nature. It created such a revealing and overwhelming iconography that it is impossible to look at it without being puzzled by the grotesqueness of an imagery that was totally accepted within the most sublime expression of religion – the Gothic cathedrals. More importantly, this imagery was accepted by the collective consciousness of that time.

To go back even farther, the archives of the Warburg Institute in London have a reproduction of an ancient image showing a mother offering her child to Priapus. We could call it a sort of 'baptism.' Perhaps this kind of thing happened at a time when culture knew more about being the child of a particular god, when we could say baptism was more differentiated, expressing an acceptance of being connected to the god one was a child of. I am not interested

Plate 10

Loco picaro

Plate 11

Plate 12

in 'proving' the evidence of the reproduction which I found by chance. From the psychological point of view, it is enough if someone conceived a baptism to Priapus.

With the reappearance of the freak today under a new historical enactment, and society's increased tolerance towards it, people are expressing openly freakish elements that only yesterday belonged to the realm of the outcast or the institution. The way in which the new historical appearance of this side of the archetype makes it possible to carry a pathology is worth mentioning in our study of imagery. As Jung said, though in a different context: had it not been for the many religious sects, theosophy, spiritualism, astrology, etc., we would need more mental institutions than we have. I would like to go further and add to these more openly paranoid systems the living reality of the freak who, as a way of life within a borderline, carries what otherwise would be considered a pathology, a borderline pathology. Or, to be more precise, this archetypal complex can evoke a picture of how a pathology is lived within a condition which otherwise would need to be institutionalized.

We can detect the freakishness among religious leaders, politicians, scientists, royal families, as well as in a Swiss banker or the most true-blue psychologist. This detection can be considered a gain in our psychological awareness and, thanks to this god, it seems to be expanding to the advantage of psychology. To become acquainted with the imagery of freakishness, either in the body or in a way of life, is indeed a gain. In both cases a pathology is expressed but, at the same time, its imagery, in spite of being disguised by other archetypes, tells us vividly about this intrinsic aspect of human nature we call freakish.

There is an even more important aspect in today's awareness of the freak in others and in oneself, more important from a psychotherapeutic point of view. It is when the patient is able to detect the freakishness in the parental situation. This attitude has been taken as an aggressive attitude toward the parental *imago*. However, archetypally speaking, it is a valid connection to the parents, a connection expressed within the situation of the family pathology. I would tend to see it as yet another borderline carrying new values into psychotherapy. Here I would like to mention the stereotyped analytical attitude coined as the 'restoration of the parental *imago*,' a fantasy which pushes the psychotherapist into trying to play the parental role and thus falsifying psychotherapy. This conceptualized notion, coming from Western culture's fantasy of patriarchal seriousness, leaves out what sometimes seems to me the deeper, more therapeutically useful connection of Hermes and, in this case, Priapus, who I am trying to equate with the freak.

For furthering our imagery of Priapus the Freak, let us turn to a classical book which gives us a vivid picture of the life of Priapus' children. *The Satyricon*[9] was written by Petronius during the time of Nero, a very freakish time indeed. The title is said to be taken from an aphrodisiac herb called *satyrion*.[10] Unfortunately, the book has come down to us badly fragmented, and this makes the reading of it somewhat tiresome and unsatisfactory. There are, however, translations which attempt to give the book more coherence by filling in the gaps between the fragments, such as the translation published at the beginning of the century and attributed to Oscar Wilde[11]; it is one of the versions I have used in this study.

The version which triggered my imagination the most concerning Priapus was Federico Fellini's film *Satyricon*, a masterpiece of image-making. He borrowed from the classical book those elements akin to him, but also filled in the gaps with images of his own. Not only do his images make for more coherence, but due to his genius, they are extraordinarily true to the archetypal situation of the children of Priapus. He made this film within an entirely pagan concep-

9. Petronius, *The Satyricon and the Fragments*, trans. J.P. Sullivan (Penguin: Hammondsworth, 1965).
10. *Ibid.*, p. 184, fn. 15.
11. *The Satyricon of Petronius*, trans. "Sebastian Melmoth," MCMII.

tion, uncontaminated by the Christian standpoint, something we must recognize as a tremendous achievement.

The book hints at the secret cults of Priapus. (Petronius records that there were about a thousand worshippers of Priapus, from all classes of society. We have to be careful about placing this archetype within a social substrata as it could be misleading, as is the tendency to see the picaresque and the trickster in the same way. In the third chapter, our heroes – Ascyltos, Encolpius, and Giton – trespass into a shrine of Priapus, thereby creating some confusion among the worshippers. A little later, we realize that what could be called irreverent behavior toward a god was used by Quartilla, a priestess of Priapus, as a pretext to push our heroes into an orgy. As we go on with the text of the story, we get an impression of the worshipping of this peculiar god, which includes an orgy of the priestess, her slaves, the worshippers, and the intruders. All this confusion seems to be part of the constellation of the god.

Both the film and the book show the ups and downs in the sexual rivalry between Encolpius and Ascyltos over Giton, also the ups and downs of a sexuality in which there is a constant longing for potency (the *satyrion* herb) but which, in reality, shows impotence and weakness. There are scenes of ridiculous jealousy, promises of loyalty, cheating, thieving, suicidal attempts, sexual acts performed in front of a Roman authority, as well as 'group sex.' The core of their life seems to have nothing to do with what we call dignity. We can view it as a life that expresses the undignified side of Hermes acted out through Priapus. It is an apparently gay life, full of awkwardness and oddities, poetry and art, in which is reflected the peculiar way the children of Priapus live their sexuality. These and other scenes express the need for an extreme sexuality within the imagery appropriate for these children of Priapus. Their longing for sexual potency reminds us of the ithyphallic aspect of Hermes and the crooked phallus of Priapus, and both images help us to see the weakening. The children of Priapus are weak, even within the potency that some of their sexual fantasies claim;

it is the weakening which is the result of the Hermaphrodite, whether it appears as a consciousness, a psychic mover,
or is acted out through the body.

We meet this strange erotica in psychotherapy in cases
where the Priapic component dominates. It is an erotica
that in its heterosexual, but, even more, in its homosexual
manifestation is full of demands and constant complaints
about the sexual relationship; relationships, like that of our
heroes in *Satyricon,* packed with foolish, strange jealousy,
spiteful envy, and in which any dialogue about the relationship is full of mutual bitchery. Usually, with this rather
common patient, the therapist sees the sentimental and
sometimes pathetic messes they bring into psychotherapy as
inherited from the parental complexes and tries to heal
these complexities causalistically. On the other hand, these
sort of patients, particularly if they are overtly homosexual,
offer a unique opportunity to look through the messes they
bring with them – situations full of childish claims, hysterical
anxieties, and endless psychopathic repetitions of the same
scene in life – as the expression *in vivo* of an archetype.
These patients offer an archetypal image in its own physical
body expression which, one is tempted to say, reveals trans-
parently the alchemical, biological nature of the archetype,
a nature it would be foolish to attribute only to the personal
history of the patient.[12] However, one can say it is a nature
which seeks a personal history in accordance with its own
peculiarity. The view I am trying to expand here is crucial
for an archetypally oriented psychology, which inclines
towards having an intuition of which archetype is predominant in the construction of a personality. It involves having

12. The point I want to stress is that with the freakish Priapic patient we
are given the opportunity to see through, hermetically, into deeper
levels of an archetypal nature, into its oddity, that other patients – the
so-called "normal neurotics" – do not propitiate; except perhaps for
the puer aeternus, whose archetypal nature is dominated by fantasies
of flying. With the Priapic patient, the constellation is very different to
that of the puer, since the former evokes some repulsion, even with an
analyst accustomed to this imagery.

an intuitive look into what is seemingly a very strange nature and respecting it. Any reduction to a life's trauma or to the parental relationship and education can only be short-sighted or a safe retreat into terminology.

Some lines in the book particularly caught my attention. It is the part where Petronius lets us know that Encolpius feels himself persecuted by Priapus: "Over land and white Nereus' sea, I am hounded / By the mighty rage of Priapus of Hellespont."[13] These lines allow us to touch upon that very frequent dream motif of the dreamer being persecuted by a figure which, in Jungian psychotherapy, has tended to be seen as a shadow figure. Petronius offers some differentiation; Priapus can persecute, and Encolpius becomes impotent. In his prayer, Encolpius refers to other persecutions, an important motif in classical literature, for example: the persecution of Ulysses by Poseidon. In the *Satyricon* the persecution motif and its pathology is evident: The text tells us that the healing of Encolpius' 'illness,' his impotence, a condition attributed to Priapus, was accomplished by Hermes.

The last scene of Fellini's film gives us the impression that our hero, Encolpius, has somehow given a response to the persecution of Priapus, that a 'process' has been going on. We see him in solitude within a fitting scenery. He is in profound reflection and through this conveys to the audience that he seems to have absorbed all that has happened to him. The component figures of his life come out of his soul now as memory-images, a memory seen by Fellini in the beauty of a Roman mosaic, its many pieces very well placed.

Fellini connects vividly to the concretized hermaphroditism of the children of Priapus, in the claim to be Hermaphroditus himself. He turns the Lichas episode on the ship into a pederast's wedding, certainly a freakish business and something we have already seen in the painting by Ribera and to which I shall return. Another episode in the film expresses this concretization superbly, though from a differ-

13. Petronius, *The Satyricon and the Fragments, op. cit.*, p. 160.

ent angle. It is the scene where the Hermaphrodite, portrayed as a frail albino child, is worshipped in a very odd way by the most freakish children of the god. The two heroes – Encolpius and Ascyltos – make the ultimate concretization of stealing this strange healing power as a fetish and for a picaresque profit, an act that inevitably leads to its destruction.

This fetishist, concretized side of the Hermaphrodite has appeared in modern psychotherapy. Psychotherapists, both men and women, express a concretized bodily manifestation of Hermaphroditus, very different, as has been stressed before, from the hermaphroditic consciousness we discussed in the first chapter. Priapus' claim to be Hermaphroditus should be seen as a different transferential need and urgency than that of Ovid's Hermaphroditus. Both these images of the Hermaphrodite have their own psychological value, both help us to see, diagnose and mark the transferential process and healing. From the psychotherapeutical point of view, we have to accept the hermaphroditism of Priapus as being centered in that confusion of being sometimes the father, sometimes the son of Hermes, the legacy of his three other fathers – Dionysus, Adonis, and Zeus – with Aphrodite always as his mother. It seems to be that any healing is within this confusion.

In *Giulietta degli Spiriti,* Fellini reflects this concretized hermaphroditism in a scene in which he introduces a woman psychotherapist with the hermaphroditism of a manly body and stereotyped ideas about group therapy, delivered in a gruff voice with a strong Northern European accent. This image, captured by Fellini's eye, stimulates one to try to figure out just exactly how healing is procured at this level. My suggestion is that she procures healing precisely through the freakishness of her body – that concretized manifestation of the Hermaphrodite – because it is impossible to imagine any healing in the boring, horrifying jargon she spouts, a mixed salad of pseudo ideas (pseudo logos) of a woman who, in classic Jungian terms, would be seen as an extreme case of animus possession.

Priapus has a healing aspect (in the days of his cult, according to the book, he used to heal impotence as well as the ague), and we are striving to arrive at the idea that his healing function lies precisely in the peculiarity of his image, expressed *through the body and its movements* which, most of the time, seem very odd. In his film, *Amarcord,* Fellini offers another insight of this sort. He shows a mad-man in the top of a tree, shouting his need for a woman for hours and hours, completely oblivious of any attempt to get him down. (Needless to say, his family is very upset and confused.) But finally he is easily subdued by a tiny, dwarf-like, freakish nun. It is a scene that routs any attempt to rationalize it, but which is, nevertheless, a readable image. It seems to me that the connection between the possible healing of the lady therapist in *Giulietta degli Spiriti* and the rather freakish little nun, who can subdue a madman simply by her presence, is that both belong within the archetypal appearance of the freak.

From a psychotherapeutic point of view, Priapus offers our imagination a hermaphroditism which, because of that claim to be Hermaphroditus himself, is a concretized fan-tasy expressed in the body, i.e., our lady therapist and the little nun. And it is perhaps this hermaphroditic body which constellates a Priapic transference in psychotherapy. For there is evidence of transference in the two examples.

Evidently Fellini has a special gift for the making of Priapic freakish images, that are such a feature of his films. Moreover, he accompanies his images with the psychology pertaining to them. All the images he has contributed amplify and make up a memory-catalogue of many aspects of the freak, his madness, and way of life. Two of his later films compliment the classical image of Priapus – that phallic scarecrow with a huge tongue and mighty belly – and allow me to refer specifically to the huge tongue. In *Casanova,* there is a scene in which a group of very austere, religious, Castilian, wealthy tourists (as I imagine them), all dressed in black, have been invited to an eighteenth-century pornographic live-show: a banquet followed by a theatrical performance by their host, dressed in a gorgeous turquoise blue with little butterfly wings, personifying Psyche, and a beautiful boy, personifying Eros. They perform the myth of Eros and Psyche within an eighteenth-century imagination, the central feature being the huge tongue of Priapus constantly flicking in and out of Psyche's mouth. The Spanish 'tourists' sit frozen in their prudery. In *Rehearsal of an Orchestra,* a young woman musician enters the hall who brings together her virtuosity as a flautist with the power of her tongue.

Now, for the image that enabled me to see a depth in what, externally, seems merely a process through oddities, let us return to *The Satyricon.* In Petronius' book, with its detailed description, and Fellini's film, with its plasticity, the center of the action is Trimalchio's feast. This masterpiece of a scene conveys all the grotesqueness, bad taste, oddity, and freakishness of a Roman banquet. There are basically four courses (though they seem endless). Let us just mention here the stuffed boiled calf and the pastry Priapus. This exaggerated and grotesque food is eaten during foolish discussions about astrology, the making of a free man out of a slave, what it is to be a poor man, salted with many puns and inaccurate mythology and erudition. We discover Trimalchio's history through the gossip of his guests and also his own recounting of how he made his fortune and became a free man. There is his grotesque behavior with his slaves, his playing with little boys in front of his wife and her jealousy, etc., which could be taken as a classic example of the behavior of a child of Priapus. It is a dinner accompanied by many orgiastic and sexual oddities. But this is not all. At the conclusion of the feast, Trimalchio reads his will and epitaph amidst the weeping of himself and his household. In the book, he discusses the construction of his tomb and then lies on a couch while a funeral dirge is played. In the film, he leads his guests in a procession to visit the tomb he has already built, where, in front of them all, he proves the correctness of its measurement.

Trimalchio's, what might be called, obsession with his own death and funeral hints at what is behind the façade presented by this child of Priapus – nouveau riche, longing for pleasure, overtly sexual, his desire to impress, etc. For, at the same time, his sexual fantasies and eating, taken to their final consequences, are leading to the realm of the dead, the Underworld, but this is expressed by way of the concretization so characteristic of the children of Priapus. Spanish history commonly tells that Charles V, when retired to the monastery at Yuste, used to rehearse his funeral by fitting himself into his coffin.

Spanish tradition has viewed this enactment of a death imagery as a touch of mysticism in a man who had ruled an enormous empire and then, in order to retire and wait for death, passed it on to his son. The tale belongs to the Spanish tradition's wealth of images of death. However, that the most powerful ruler in Europe retired to a monastery in Estremadura to wait for his death, with that touch of humility and mysticism so intrinsic to the Spanish soul, is only one side of the coin. The other side tells us that Charles V was bored with ruling Spain and not much interested in his vast empire, nor was he concerned with culture, but was plagued with a constant nostalgia for his days in Flanders, where he ate and drank in the taverns. He chose Yuste as his place of retirement, first, because the Geronimus Order of monks was well-known for its excellent cooking and, secondly, because Yuste was situated fairly close to the sea. So, from Flanders, he used to receive consignments of lobsters, herrings, soles, etc., and beer. At the end of the last century, Castelar wrote an article about the gluttony of Charles V, which Xavier Domingo comments on in his book, *La Mesa del Buscon:*

> Apart from the fantastic daily menu, Charles V had always at hand a ham from Montánchez and at various times of the day he would pick at slices of that delicious meat whose quality was attributed to the fact that the pigs of that region ate a great quantity of vipers and snakes.[14]

In my own experience, during a Pantagruelian lunch, a poet, who really enjoyed eating, in a beautiful poetic line expressed a peculiar sort of ecstasy combining eating and death, which I attribute to the children of Priapus: "A horcajadas del borde de la cazuela Barroca hasta la muerte."[15] His poetic genius expressed the freakishness in eating and took it to the final consequence of death. This man was a freak and a great poet. We have to question whether artists, who live their freakishness and oddness, are possibly more able to reflect this archetype in life. Jung said the artist's task is to compensate the collective consciousness, which leads us to ask whether it is not the artist's expression of freakishness, and the freakish lives of some of them, that has in fact compensated the collective consciousness throughout history. Certainly freakishness in art allows a reflection of this archetype which, with all its distortions, procures psychic movement, humanness, and depth.

In both the poet's eating and the way he described it, and the rehearsals with their tombs of Trimalchio and Charles V, there is a body activity in which bodily expression and imagination are one and the same. They are activating their imagination (active imagination), activating images that have to do with death, an imaginative activity which is suggestive for the appearance of images of death in psychotherapy: Hermes as Priapus connecting two extremes of the soul – a freakish eating, with its attachment to life, and depression and death. Here again we find Hermes with his ithyphallic sexuality, lord of the roads, leading the freakish children of his son, by acting out the imagination, to a connection with the realm of depression and death.

This could be a challenge for Jung's followers, who prefer to conceive of 'active imagination' as a stereotyped method of conversing with images in the unconscious. The

14. Xavier Domingo, *La Mesa del Buscon* (Tusquets Editores: Barcelona, 1981), p. 30 (trans. mine).
15. Translated literally, this means "Straddling the rim of a Baroque earthenware cooking pot until death."

three 'active imaginations' of Trimalchio, Charles V and a great poet imply a connection with their depression, a side of the psyche which should not be forgotten by the practitioners of active imagination. The appearance of an imagery of death in psychotherapy is always welcome to a psychotherapist who knows how essential it is for the psyche's life.

But here my concern is to discuss the active imagination of the children of Priapus, because it is indeed an active imagination, *but through the body*. It is the image expressed by way of a bodily performance or, you could say, the 'acting out' of the image. Another way of putting it would be to say that Trimalchio is enacting the rhetoric pertaining to Priapus. However, the conception of rhetoric in relation to archetypes is as yet a latent possibility awaiting further study. It has potential also for psychotherapists who are interested in exploring the rhetoric of each archetype and who can insight and integrate it into their psychotherapeutic conception and practice.

We cannot call this active imagination a theater because it is not the performing of a part, or a role. Nor can we call it a psychodrama because it is not the enactment of a past episode in a life. I prefer to regard it as an active imagination stemming from an archetypal connection to Priapus, which can lay a favorable ground for a psychotherapy with a spectrum that spans from the image to a body enactment.

Before continuing, I would like to come back to the previous discussion in relation to Pan. If in the constellation of Pan the body seeks a symmetry in words (through Echo) and movements between analyst and patient, in relation to Priapus the elements of body expression are different: the memories of the pieces of our historical complexes are moved, or removed, through the spontaneity of the imagination enacted through the body, with a speech backed by the rhetoric of Priapus. Once more we can detect the total failure of the concept, interpretation, or amplification when Priapus/freak is constellated. The psychotherapeutic answer is our body expression. We do absolutely nothing by sitting in a chair 'interpreting' the 'material,' for this archetype demands something else. The challenge for the analyst is to be and act within the constellation, to be aware of body-movements which are freakish, and to revalue these elements, so undignified that they tend to be outcast. I am referring here to the complexes connected to the archetype of Priapus, and his father, or son Hermes – they are indeed undignified. The response to the epiphany of Priapus, as I would like to understand this archetypal complex, is to enact the freak in psychotherapy, to hold and recognize the freak with all its awkwardness, poetry, and healing.

I recall a gifted psychotherapist, no doubt living within that borderline necessary for this constellation, who practised clinical psychotherapy with a severely depressed patient by fantasizing freakishly about his own depression. In this way he was able to give the right dosage of what were, evidently, images very alien to a depressed Herr Professor. The reader might choose to see this as a compensatory psychotherapy; or it can be seen as a happening, acted out in the archetypal configuration of the freakish Priapus.

Another psychotherapeutic approach of this psychotherapist was to move in front of a schizophrenic girl with body movements which reminded me of Jacques Tati in his masterwork, *Les Vacances de Monsieur Hulot;* this also reminds us of the close archetypal connection of the Priapic approach to the fool and the comedian. Possibly the rigidity of her illness was moved indirectly through his body movements. As is well-known, this element of body movement is most important in psychotherapy with psychotic and borderline cases. It is a movement of the body which, in this case, I associate with Priapus.

Now let us turn to the contemporary American scene. It is more familiar to us and will, perhaps, help to further our view of the freakish side of life, and give us an impression of how alive Priapus is today. The films of Andy Warhol give us more ingredients to add to our picture of the children of Priapus. Take, for instance, *Trash:* The hero of this film is a drug addict who lives with a transvestite, a situation that is a variation of what we have seen before in the painting of

Ribera and Fellini's Lichas episode. *Trash* portrays very well the characteristic sexuality of the children of Priapus. Predominant is that mixture of extreme sexual urgency and impotence. However, it was a scene in another Warhol film that gave me the image from which to approach the rhetoric of Priapus, an aspect which complements the body movement we are concerned with. It is a certain kind of speech that seems to me very freakish and has to do with the children of Priapus. The scene I am about to describe can help us to become acquainted with a way of talking which, from my experience, opens up possibilities for psychotherapy.

It is a famous scene with one of Warhol's Superstars. She is standing in a kitchen in front of a man and, while slowly removing her clothes, she rambles on in a sort of long monologue on the subject of eggs: how to cook eggs – you can poach eggs; you can boil eggs; fry eggs; eggs are nice in an omelette and, to make it more tasty, you can put in a bit of ham, etc. We are reminded a bit of that silly conversation during Trimalchio's banquet, apparently so superficial and stupid but which, as far as I can see, has to do with the style of speech of the children of Priapus, or what we want to arrive at as the rhetoric of Priapus. But the point I would like to stress is that the appearance of this kind of speech in psychotherapy, with all its superficiality, repetitive stupidity, and banality is part of the constellation of Priapus, comes from this god and is what propitiates him. If, in psychotherapy, we are in the happening of Priapus, then inevitably, our way of talking has to be within the constellation, our speech also has to be Priapic. We cannot talk with the articulate jargon ascribed to the schools of psychology, nor ask questions with the purpose of tracking down conflicts and traumas, etc. Conceptions do not belong at all to this archetype.

Let me illustrate what I am trying to get at with the case of a fourteen-year-old boy who came for therapy. It was easy to see that he was persecuted by Priapus. His main symptom was a fear of being touched on the bottom by someone in the street, in school, or in a queue, etc. He was obsessed by his sexuality, by pornography, and whether he would ever be able to have sex one day. During the first hour, he asked me if I knew of a brothel for children. However, during most of the psychotherapy, I used to spend hours in dialogues like this:

Why do you smoke Marlboro cigarettes?
Well, because they are not bad.

What's the cigarette your wife smokes?
Well, she smokes Astors.

Do you like Winstons?
Sometimes, sometimes I smoke Winstons.

But you don't like menthol cigarettes?
No, no, I'm sorry, I don't like menthol cigarettes.

Well then, do you like black cigarettes?
Oh yes, I like black cigarettes when they are good, when they are tasty.

What kind of cigarette did you smoke in Europe?
Well, in Europe, I smoked Peter Stuyvesants.

But did you smoke other cigarettes as well?
Yes. Sometimes I liked to change to Gauloise.

Have you smoked German cigarettes?
No.

English?
Yes ... etc., etc.

And more or less the same sort of conversation about cars:

Why don't you have a car?
I am afraid of driving a car in Caracas.

But if you did buy a car, what sort would you like? A Mustang?
No. I like Mustangs, but that's not a car for me.

> *A station wagon?*
>> Well, maybe. Station wagons are very useful and handsome, too ... etc.

Perhaps the reader is irritated by my introducing this very tiresome, silly dialogue, but this silliness and stupidity belongs to the archetype, which expresses itself in this way. As far as I can see, what we could call a boring repetition belongs precisely to the rhetoric of Priapus and, in the case of the fourteen-year-old boy, proved to be the vehicle that caused the psychotherapeutic indirection to move within the constellation of Priapus, thus procuring the healing. To call this kind of dialogue an unconscious one is only to tell part of the story, because to call unconscious something we have already detected as belonging to the expression of an archetype is invalid from the point of view of an archetypal consciousness, which seeks to look through the psychotherapeutic constellation to the archetype constellated. I merely offer this dialogue as a point of departure for further psychological exploration.

This case offered me the opportunity to value the speech, behavior, and psychodynamic of this kind of Priapic personality. I can only imagine the psychodynamic of his sexual imagery – a brothel for children – was the expression of a need for initiation into sexuality outside the norms of the collective. We can go so far as to presume that biological complexities were probably touched through what, in the first instance, seems a silly superficial dialogue. Previously I referred to the freak as a body-image, the paradigm being the overt homosexual freak; but this was not the case with the fourteen-year-old boy, whose body appearance was 'normal,' even handsome, and who had achieved a very imaginative heterosexual erotica. His freakishness was expressed through his speech, thus procuring an insight into different strata of the archetype. In the overtly homosexual case, the body-image predominates, which, one could say, is more powerful than speech; but in the boy's case the connection to the archetypal image was definitely through speech.

There is another American film, more on the level of the daily news, which offers yet another variation on our theme. It is called *Dog Day Afternoon*. It concerns a bank robbery which actually took place. Almost from the start we realize that the bank robbers are quite different from the usual sort. They turn out to be hopelessly inefficient and weak, exhibiting some of the weakness we have mentioned before; for instance, the weakness of the heroes in Fellini's *Satyricon* after their attempt to rob the Hermaphrodite. These bank robbers obviously feel terribly embarrassed once they engage in the action of robbing the bank. Later on we discover that the motive for the robbery was to get money for today's fashionable and most freakish operation of all, the transsexual operation. Our hero, the bank robber, has previously married a homosexual who now wants this operation. And to our astonishment, it was a real wedding performed by a true-blue minister. I shall refer to this intervention of the minister later on. For now, let us remain with the transsexual operation.

Ten years ago, when this book first came out, the transsexual operation was very fashionable. To refer to it historically in terms of decades: the transsexual operation was front-page news during the seventies; but I do not think it is so fashionable today in the second half of the eighties. However, there is another worldwide appearance of Priapus and very much front-page news: coca, a South American plant that was processed into a drug during the last century. After the discovery of cocaine, it lay dormant, so to speak, and was the concern of minorities, but then, in the eighties, cocaine jumped into the front row and is now used by an ever growing number of people. These people have made it into one of the most profitable businesses on earth, the worried concern of governments and the medical profession. But nothing has been mentioned, in relation to the paraphernalia of cocaine, as to how it works in the psyche archetypally. In fact it works through Priapus, spreading the same psychodynamic we have been discussing: extreme sexual urgency and impotence. It is well-known that, in most cases, cocaine provokes an odd Priapic dichotomy between the urgency of a very activated and accelerated *fantasia sexualis* difficult to attain in the reality of the sexual body.[16]

Perhaps it could be thought in this respect that I am departing from whatever we call psychology, but let us remember we are studying an archetype whose characteristics are very odd indeed and always include a peculiar concrete aspect. With this matter of the transsexual operation and cocaine, we are concerned with two of the most extreme appearances of the archetype in today's world.

In 1973 I was fortunate in having the opportunity to talk about this operation with Dr. Merrill, a urologist, who works in collaboration with a psychiatrist, Dr. Markland, in Minnesota. At the time I met them they had performed twenty-five operations of this kind. They consider that the men who ask for this operation belong to a group apart from the homosexual criterion. They are patients who express concretely that they are really a woman trapped in a man's body. This is the criterion for selecting the candidates for the operation, and this psychiatric criterion appears in *Dog Day Afternoon*.

There is a well-known illness which takes its name from Priapus – Priapism. This rare illness manifests itself in men who, supposedly, have had a very vigorous sexual life. But when the illness hits, it turns the vigorous sexuality into what physicians familiar with it call an impotent erection, a condition requiring an operation called Caverno Spongious Shunt. Through this connection I was able to talk with some post-surgical patients of Priapism. One has the same picture of those extremes of potency and irreparable weakness. To one's amazement, they have no sexual fantasies and, if one

16. For those interested in cocaine in relation to the history of modern psychology, see Sigmund Freud, *The Cocaine Papers*, Ed. and Intrd. Robert Byck, M.D. (Meridian, New American Library: New York, 1975), which includes notes by Anna Freud, Freud's correspondence, and other papers on cocaine.

hints at sexual fantasies, their immediate reaction is that they have an absolutely 'normal' sexuality. They repeat the word 'normal' in a tremendously convincing way. During the conversations with these patients there was little or nothing I could gather to put me on the track of any movement towards what we call a psychical sexuality, or memories of sexual images. I had no impression of a life's tragedy, or drama, or even of a disturbed sexuality; only that constant repetition of the word 'normal.' "I am perfectly normal," "I have always had a very normal sexuality," etc.

But there was something more, something I would like to add to the language or rhetoric of the children of Priapus. One patient told me about his sexuality only in terms of times and time. It was always normal. It could be two or three times or four times a week. It lasted sometimes for two hours, or two and a half hours; sometimes four hours, or five hours, sometimes six hours, or six and a half hours. I would like to add his language to the rhetoric of Priapus we are tracking down, to the dialogue with the fourteen-year-old boy, to Andy Warhol's Superstar and to the conversation during Trimalchio's feast.

Unfortunately, there is next to no training[17] for a psycho-therapeutic approach which can free us enough to give a response to the archetype of Priapus. So the response of a general psychiatrist to that most freakish case of someone wanting a transsexual operation is: "He is normal; the only thing is that the patient wants to become a woman." And by 'normal,' he means that the patient doesn't offer any of the psychiatric symptoms he is accustomed to, the symptoms he has learned about in the textbooks of modern psychopa-thology. It would seem that psychiatrists are not trained to see the oddities outside the frame of reference of their studies. To put cases like this into the framework of modern psychopathology, whether the personality is predominantly

17. Jung hinted at a psychotherapy of the body in *Mysterium Conjunctionis* and earlier in seminars on the Kundalini Yoga (see *Spring:* An Annual of Archetypal Psychology and Jungian Thought, 1975 and 1976).

ruled by Priapus or the occasional freak-out of the so-called normal neurotic, is reductive, misleading, and has nothing to do with a psychotherapeutical approach. Viewed from the psychiatric standpoint, my fourteen-year-old boy was prone for a diagnosis of paranoid persecution mania, to be subjected to inadequate treatment and a bad prognosis. Probably the difficulty is that Priapus manifests in oddities of the body and in peculiarities that are 'far out,' and have not been discussed much in modern psychology.

Perhaps these extreme cases of Priapism and the trans-sexual operation I have referred to will help us to detect the archetype and help us to develop a keener eye for recognizing its appearance in psychotherapy. Also, we might begin to reflect upon the tendency of modern psychology during this century, though more acutely recently, to be overly concerned with impotence, frigidity, orgasm, 'normal' sexuality, etc., and with an extreme and concretized emphasis on sexuality with which this god archetypally expresses himself. We are led into speculating whether psychologists are at all aware of the unconscious projections the archetype of Priapus is producing in them. In other words, one is amazed at the many therapies of today that are oriented into direct sexuality, therapies caught by Priapus. It would be interesting, from a historical point of view, to track down the way in which the imagery of Priapus – the influence of the Priapic complexes which we visualize mythologically in a trio of Hermes, Priapus, and Aphrodite – appeared among the pioneers of modern psychology in the Vienna School, the cradle of the sexology plaguing today's psychotherapy.

For a psychotherapeutic approach to the rhetoric of Priapus – to come back to the training side – the only training would be to pay attention to one's own freakishness (how freakish we are!) and to keep learning from what the artists of all times contribute to the training of our retina. And we cannot approach the rhetoric of Priapus psychotherapeutically in terms of a technique to be learned, but more as an instrument of the imagination. We all know that modern psychology began in Queen Victoria's quiet times, with a practice based on the anonymity of the analyst and patient and the tools of the couch and the chair. These remain in the conception of many analysts today, including Jungians, who are still hesitating over whether to take Jung's teachings as a fixed method, or even whether to regress to the couch situation. In any event, very few go through one of the many doors Jung opened into new psychotherapeutic adventures, into what might even be the adventure of their own individuation. In the case of Priapus, that would involve responding to the demand for an understanding of this archetype, which seems to be constellated not only in the personal constellation of the patient, but collectively in our historical times.

If the freakish aspect of life is not included in the training of modern psychotherapy, and if archetypal aspects of the personality are still seen under the view of psychiatry's classic coinages, so in Jungian psychology these aspects of the personality tend to go equally unrecognized, even if marvelously touched upon by Jung. For example, to take the tenth plate in *The Psychology of the Transference* as Jung worked it out, we read that the completion of the Hermaphrodite was seen from its symbolic side [Plate 13]. But for us, in looking at this plate again just as an image, we can easily detect a strong freakish element. The freakishness in the image probably expresses the same freakishness that was historically accepted by the Gothic Medieval man in his religious life, but now in the alchemical treatise it appears at a more personal level. To include its freakish grotesqueness when imagining the image of the tenth plate, would be, for me, to broaden Jung's view. He saw it as a realization in the transferential process leading to: "… the existing symbols, 'wholeness,' 'self,' 'consciousness,' 'higher ego,' or what you will, it makes little difference."[18] But now what we are after is a connection to the 'monstrous,' the freakish, aspect of the image and, without denying its symbolic side, a reading of the image with the added ingredient of seeing it

18. *CW* 16, para. 573.

PHILOSOPHORVM.

Plate 13

in terms of all the freakishness we have been working out in this chapter. If Jung's interpretation of the image is conflictive, it was also conflictive for the alchemist who conceived it, and it will continue to be conflictive for anyone who tries to explore it for psychology.

If we include Priapus in the tenth image of the Rosarium that opens, at least for me, the possibility of connecting to, or if you prefer, 'integrating,' elements which have a specific archetypal background: our freakishness. The freakish side of human nature is archetypal and all the elements of being both the father and son of Hermes, claiming to be a Hermaphroditus and, in the tenth image of the Rosarium, a meeting of this claim with Luna, belong within the archetypal spectrum of Priapus. There was a time when freakishness had its own religious cult and way of life; since then, it has moved here and there on the historical stage of Western culture, until its recent appearance in the world of today. It is so overwhelmingly apparent that our fantasy is moved into conceiving it as a reenactment of the old religious cult that, historically, has been so repressed. Now this religion, because it is religious, also appears front-stage in today's religious man. For example, during a Jesuit's breakdown, he let me know how persecuted he was by the fixed idea that he was a Hermaphrodite. He had tried to find a concrete diagnosis for his fantasy by consulting many different doctors – internists, endocrinologists, radiologists, etc. The archetype was apparent also in the detailed way he used to explain to me the crooked erection of his penis, an erection to the rear.

We can detect Priapus, the freak, in a clear-cut, athletic minister who hurls himself desperately into a Jungian analysis hoping that psychotherapy can fulfill his claim for wholeness. And we are reminded, too, of the minister in *Dog Day Afternoon* who married the two men.

The manifestation of Priapus makes this archetype a psychotherapeutic reality, if we are able to respond when an archetype, so freakish in its imagery, demands our attention. As far as Jung's legacy is concerned, we can now

include in it a realm of the psyche that expresses itself
through an imagery of sexuality and oddity, often upsetting
in its grotesqueness. Jungian psychotherapy is conceived
from the point of view of individuation – a very personal and
varied conception; at the same time, it is a psychotherapy
based on the compensatory function of the psyche. We
know that Hermes, because of his particular psychic nature,
and his many and odd manifestations (such as Priapus),
compensates and so balances the psyche. We could say that
he personifies the principle of compensation. It is undoubtedly because of this aspect that Jung equated him with the
self. Among Jung's contributions, the most direct and evident was his view of the onesidedness of modern man's life.
Keeping this thought in mind, I believe the reader can
become reconciled to the sometimes strange and odd imagery this book has offered. It is an imagery coming from the
more repressed side of man's psychic nature, the side where
the images reside that most compensate the dullness and
repetitive superficiality implicit in his onesidedness.

Afterword

A few last words:

First, to thank Hermes, this very psychic and evasive god, for his contribution to this work.

The reader, I believe, now has a notion of the many ways in which Hermes can contribute to the adventure of psychotherapy. It is a contribution far removed from the many psychologies of today, which try to feed psychotherapy with their theories and concepts. Hermes has his own borderline attitude to psychotherapy: he is able to barter with and connect to very alien aspects of the psyche. He can help to make an image of each psychic event the therapist is confronted with, aiding the work of the psychotherapist as image-maker. Hermes' rhetoric is conducive to the essential uniqueness of each psychotherapeutic constellation, to the therapist's response, attitude, and style, helping him to avoid falling into the trap of collective conceptions of psychotherapy. In this context, the psychotherapist's individuation can be seen as a Hermes' intervention. The spontaneity of his primitive instinct brings profoundly psychic reflections into the here and now of psychotherapy, propitiating access to deeper levels of the psyche; as we have seen, even when his rhetoric seems superficial and repetitive, Hermes is always profound.

And, finally, I would like to thank the reader for accompanying me in following Hermes down the many roads of psychotherapy.

List of Illustrations

Rafael López-Pedraza
Cultural Anxiety

Four brilliant essays by the author of *Hermes and His Children* hailing the elemental force of the irrational in a world that is all too often 'explained' and 'understood':

- Moon Madness-Titanic Love
- Cultural Anxiety
- Reflections on the *Duende*
- Consciousness of Failure.

López-Pedraza passionately urges us to acknowledge our roots in the soul and our debt to the unknowable.

150 pages, ISBN 978-3-85630-520-8

Luigi Zoja
Drugs, Addiction and Initiation
The Modern Search for Ritual

Luigi Zoja argues that the pervasive abuse of drugs in our society can in large part be ascribed to a resurgence of the collective need for initiation and initiatory structures: a longing for something sacred underlies our culture's manic drive toward excessive consumption. In a society without ritual, the drug addict seeks not so much the thrill of a high as the satisfaction of an inner need for a *participation mystique* in the dominant religion of our times: consumerism. From its critique of drug cures based on detoxification to its discussion of the esoteric-terrorist cult of the Assassins. This work is a classic in the field of psycho-anthropology.

144 pages, ISBN 978-3-85630-595-6

English Titles from Daimon

Laurens van der Post - *The Rock Rabbit and the Rainbow*
Jane Reid - *Jung, My Mother and I: The Analytic Diaries*
of Catharine Rush Cabot
R.M. Rilke - *Duino Elegies*
Miguel Serrano - *C.G. Jung and Hermann Hesse*
Helene Shulman - *Living at the Edge of Chaos*
D. Slattery / L. Corbet (Eds.) - *Depth Psychology: Meditations on the Field*
D. Slattery / G. Slater (Eds.) - *Varieties of Mythic Experience*
David Tacey - *Edge of the Sacred: Jung, Psyche, Earth*
Susan Tiberghien - *Looking for Gold*
Ann Ulanov - *Spirit in Jung*
- *Spiritual Aspects of Clinical Work*
- *Picturing God*
- *Receiving Woman*
- *The Female Ancestors of Christ*
- *The Wisdom of the Psyche*
- *The Wizards' Gate, Picturing Consciousness*
Ann & Barry Ulanov - *Cinderella and her Sisters*
- *Healing Imagination: Psyche and Soul*
Erlo van Waveren - *Pilgrimage to the Rebirth*
Eva Wertenschlag-Birkhäuser - *Windows on Eternity:*
The Paintings of Peter Birkhäuser
Harry Wilmer - *How Dreams Help*
- *Quest for Silence*
Luigi Zoja - *Drugs, Addiction and Initiation*
Luigi Zoja & Donald Williams - *Jungian Reflections on September 11*
Jungian Congress Papers - *Jerusalem 1983: Symbolic & Clinical Approaches*
- *Berlin 1986: Archetype of Shadow in a Split World*
- *Paris 1989: Dynamics in Relationship*
- *Chicago 1992: The Transcendent Function*
- *Zürich 1995: Open Questions*
- *Florence 1998: Destruction and Creation*
- *Cambridge 2001*
- *Barcelona 2004: Edges of Experience*
- *Cape Town 2007: Journeys, Encounters*

Available from your bookstore or from our distributors:

AtlasBooks
30 Amberwood Parkway
Ashland OH 44805, USA
Phone: 419-281-5100
Fax: 419-281-0200
E-mail: order@atlasbooks.com
www.AtlasBooksDistribution.com

Gazelle Book Services Ltd.
White Cross Mills, High Town
Lancaster LAI 4XS, UK
Tel: +44(0)152468765
Fax: +44(0)152463232
Email: Sales@gazellebooks.co.uk
www.gazellebooks.co.uk

Daimon Verlag - Hauptstrasse 85 - CH-8840 Einsiedeln - Switzerland
Phone: (41)(55) 412 2266   Fax: (41)(55) 412 2231
email: info@daimon.ch
Visit our website: **www.daimon.ch** *or write for our complete catalog*

Microbiology
and Infectious Disease

Microbiology and Infectious Disease

Editor
BERNARD A. BRIODY, Ph.D.
Professor and Chairman, Department of Microbiology
College of Medicine and Dentistry of New Jersey
New Jersey Medical School
Newark

Associate Editor
ROBERT E. GILLIS, D.D.S., Ph.D.
Professor and Chairman, Department of Oral Biology
College of Medicine and Dentistry of New Jersey
New Jersey Dental School;
Professor of Microbiology
New Jersey Medical School
Newark

McGRAW-HILL BOOK COMPANY
A Blakiston Publication

New York   St. Louis   San Francisco   Düsseldorf   Johannesburg   Kuala Lumpur   London   Mexico
Montreal   New Delhi   Panama   Paris   São Paulo   Singapore   Sydney   Tokyo   Toronto

This book was set in Times Roman by Rocappi, Inc.
The editors were Paul K. Schneider and Ida Abrams Wolfson;
the designer was Barbara Ellwood;
the cover was designed by Nicholas Krenitsky;
the production supervisor was Thomas J. LoPinto.
The drawings were done by Eric G. Hieber Associates, Inc.
The printer was The Murray Printing Company;
the binder, Rand McNally & Company.

Library of Congress Cataloging in Publication Data

Briody, Bernard Aloysius.
    Microbiology and infectious disease.

    Includes bibliographies.
    1. Medical microbiology. 2. Bacterial diseases.
I. Gillis, Robert E., joint author. II. Title.
[DNLM: 1. Infections. 2. Microbiology. WC100
B858m 1974]
QR46.B69   616.01   73-19880
ISBN 0-07-007910-2

NOTICE

Medicine is an ever-changing science. As new research and clinical experience broaden our knowledge, changes in treatment and drug therapy are required. The editors and the publisher of this work have made every effort to ensure that the drug dosage schedules herein are accurate and in accord with the standards accepted at the time for publication. The reader is advised, however, to check the product information sheet included in the package of each drug he plans to administer to be certain that changes have not been made in the recommended dose or in the contraindications for administration. This recommendation is of particular importance in regard to new or infrequently used drugs.

Microbiology and Infectious Disease

1 2 3 4 5 6 7 8 9 0 M U R M 7 9 8 7 6 5 4

Contents

List of Contributors

PASQUALE F. BARTELL, Ph.D.
Professor of Microbiology
College of Medicine and Dentistry of New Jersey
New Jersey Medical School, Newark

ZIGMUND C. KAMINSKI, Ph.D.
Associate Professor of Microbiology
Associate Professor of Pathology
College of Medicine and Dentistry of New Jersey
New Jersey Medical School, Newark

ARTHUR E. KRIKSZENS, Ph.D.
Assistant Professor of Microbiology
College of Medicine and Dentistry of New Jersey
New Jersey Medical School, Newark

MARVIN N. SCHWALB, Ph.D.
Assistant Professor of Microbiology
College of Medicine and Dentistry of New Jersey
New Jersey Medical School, Newark

FRANCIS E. SHOVLIN, D.D.S.
Professor and Chairman, Department of Endodontics
College of Medicine and Dentistry of New Jersey
New Jersey Dental School, Newark

Preface

The first eleven chapters of this text are concerned with (1) the structure and function of prokaryotic and eukaryotic parasites; (2) the general characteristics of bacteria, viruses, rickettsiae, chlamydiae, fungi, protozoa, and helminths with emphasis on those associated with pathogenicity for man, with the origin of new genotypes and with response to chemotherapy; (3) the attributes of the host that enable it to resist infection and selected factors that lower that resistance; (4) immunological interactions between haptens, antigens, parasites, and man; and (5) the basis of the immunological uniqueness of the individual and its significance in clinical medicine.

Emphasis in the balance of the text is placed on the disease rather than the parasite and on similar pathogenetic patterns and epidemiological phenomena rather than on the pathogenic potential and epidemiology of a specific parasite in isolation from many other parasites that can cause almost identical disease in man. Such an approach constitutes a sharp break with traditional texts in microbiology, but on the other hand, corresponds to the conventional presentation of subject matter in most medical texts (medicine, surgery, and pediatrics). In addition, an approach based on pathogenesis conforms to the natural diagnostic sequence followed by medical clerks, house officers, and practitioners in evaluating the clinical manifestations of patients.

We are committed to an analytical approach, an emphasis on mechanisms, a search for common foundations, a comprehension of significant ideas and concepts, and an awareness of the changing patterns of infectious disease. Whenever the data appear to warrant, we take a position. On the other hand, we challenge conclusions based on unconvincing evidence. In doing so we are painfully conscious of our own fallibility and the limits of most generalizations. Nonetheless, we persist in this course in an effort to illustrate how scientific information can be used to make clinical decisions.

BERNARD A. BRIODY